THE CRISTA **4** CHRONICLES

Escape of The Grizzly

Mark Littleton

HARVEST HOUSE PUBLISHERS
EUGENE, OREGON 97402

ESCAPE OF THE GRIZZLY

Copyright © 1994 by Mark Littleton
Published by Harvest House Publishers
Eugene, Oregon 97402

Library of Congress Cataloging-in-Publication Data

Littleton, Mark R., 1950–
    Escape of the grizzly / Mark Littleton.
      p.   cm. — (Crista chronicles ; bk. 4)
    Summary: When a supposedly tame grizzly bear escapes from a
nearby circus, twelve-year-old Crista becomes involved in a conflict be-
tween those who want to save him and those who want him killed.
    ISBN 1-56507-099-2
    [1. Grizzly bear—Fiction. 2. Bears—Fiction. 3. Circus—Fiction.]
I. Title. II. Series: Littleton, Mark R., 1950–
Crista chronicles series ; bk. 4.
PZ7.L7364Es   1994   93-29408
[Fic]—dc20   CIP
                                             AC

Printed in the United States of America.

94 95 96 97 98 99 00 01 — 10 9 8 7 6 5 4 3

Contents

·1·
Sirens!

Crista Mayfield and her two friends, Jeff Pallaci and Lindy Helstrom, rode down the highway, keeping to the soft shoulder. Their three horses were trotting along happily, obviously liking the chill air, their breath spraying white streams as they snorted and clopped along.

"I could do this forever," Lindy said to no one in particular.

Crista replied, "Forever's a long time."

"Then for sixty-two years." Lindy gave Crista her triumphant grin. Lindy Helstrom was a second grader whom Crista tutored after school for extra spending money and for fun. The little freckle-faced girl was a spunk. She got into plenty of trouble, but Crista had tamed her a bit over the last few months.

Crista was about to answer with something witty when suddenly a siren blared out behind them. Crowding the horses over toward the trees, the three kids stopped as the sheriff's brown car with 911 plastered on the rear end whooshed by. Dirt and dust billowed behind the wheels. Jeff yelled above the sound of the siren, "What's going on?"

"I don't know," Crista answered, shielding her eyes from the afternoon sun. "But look up ahead."

There, just beyond where the highway curved, a huge orange truck with black painted stripes like a tiger's had stopped almost in the middle of the road.

"Let's go!" Jeff shouted. Jeff Pallaci was Crista's best friend. He wore his blond hair kind of long and had gangly legs, cool green eyes, and an unswerving love for slingshots and other weapons, even though Crista rarely tolerated his playing with them when she was around. He lived down Rock Road from Crista, and they were both in the sixth grade. The two spent a lot of time together. He even helped her with Lindy, who lived down the highway on the continuation of Rock Road not far from the Wilkinses' farm, where the horses lived.

"Last one there's a rotten skunk cabbage!" Lindy yelled in response, giving Lukas, the sleepy gray stallion, a kick.

Crista watched as they both bolted forward. "All right, Betsarama," she said to the quick roan mare, "let's show them who's boss."

In less than a minute she galloped up alongside the other two. As they thundered closer to the curve, they saw other vehicles stopped behind the one with the tiger stripes. Reaching the first truck and trailer, the threesome pulled up from their gallop and stopped, gaping. There in slashes of bright colors and poster paint stood a line of 30 or more trucks, vans, trailers, and station wagons. Several policemen had parked their patrol cars on the other side of the road and people milled around, darting back and forth across the two-lane highway.

"Looks like a big accident," Jeff said, panting from the gallop. "Let's get closer."

He kicked Thunder, and the three of them trotted past the police cars. They stayed on the side opposite the colored trucks. Finally, they saw the cause of the trouble: an overturned trailer. The roof had collapsed and lay in a splintered mess in the ditch on the right-hand side of the road. The sides of the trailer splayed out in four pieces, covering half the highway. In the middle of the wreckage was a large cage. Its door was open and whatever had been inside was gone. Around the cage, which obviously the trailer had been trans-porting, a man in a pith helmet was shouting orders. Other people, including the policemen, hustled about, several of them holding shotguns.

One of the officers began directing traffic and as the threesome drew nearer, he blew a whistle at them. "Get to the side!" he shouted. "And keep moving!"

Crista led Betsarama deeper onto the brown dirt shoulder. All three of the kids turned to peer at the destroyed trailer.

"It must be a circus or something," Jeff said as he walked Thunder up next to Crista.

"Yeah, and there must have been animals in that one," Lindy replied, pointing to the overturned trailer. "It looks like it had a cage inside."

"Let's stop for a second, walk the horses, and really get a good look," Crista suggested. She pulled the reins back and Betsarama stopped. She quickly jumped down to the dirt.

The policeman behind her directing traffic yelled, "Hey, you kids, keep going! There are wild bears loose here."

"Wild bears!" Jeff cried. He looked excitedly around. Crista gripped the pommel and pulled herself back up immediately, her neck hairs prickling with fear.

Betsarama acted a bit skittish, backing up and prancing forward as Crista threw her leg over the saddle. "Easy girl," Crista said, patting her neck. "I think the horses smell the bears," she said to Jeff and Lindy.

"Yeah, I bet they're big ones, too," Jeff replied. Thunder pawed the ground and backed up, then leaped forward. "Okay, okay," Jeff said, reining in the big, black stallion. Thunder gradually came under control. Only Lukas, Lindy's horse, seemed unconcerned about the scent the other horses were getting.

Jeff caressed Thunder's neck. "I bet they're Kodiaks or big brown bears or maybe pandas or something."

"I doubt they're pandas," Crista remarked, still reining in the nervous Betsarama. "Pandas are too rare. They're probably black bears. That's what you mostly see in circuses."

Jeff pulled his ski cap up, revealing more of his light, slightly curly hair. "I've seen some pretty weird things in circuses—big mean bears, a guy putting his head in their mouths, stuff like that. It was cool."

Crista rolled her eyes. "Well, we're not putting our heads in any bear mouth."

"Yeah, they probably don't even use Listerine!" Lindy added, always one to make a joke. "Oh, look." Lindy pointed again. "The back of the trailer says, 'Daring Dan and His Three Beastly Bears.' It must be an act or something."

Crista watched as the man in the pith helmet stopped and stooped down where the tire had come off the trailer axle. Another man in overalls bent down with him and Crista heard him say, "Did you see that, Cal?"

"Yeah," the man named Cal in the pith helmet said. "Those lug nuts were tight when I last checked them."

"Well, they're gone now. And lug nuts don't come off unless someone takes them off."

"Sabotage?"

"Looks like it."

Crista turned and whispered to Jeff, "It sounds like it wasn't an accident."

"I heard," Jeff said. "Someone must have wanted this to happen."

The man named Cal stood and walked around the truck. For all the commotion about loose bears, everyone looked strangely calm, like they were waiting for something to happen.

Then it did. Some caught beast bellowed in the woods.

All three horses jumped. Jeff held in Thunder, but Betsarama darted out into the middle of the highway and turned toward home. It was all Crista could do to hold her back. Lindy sat on Lukas, though, as if she were queen for a day.

"What's the matter?" Lindy smiled sweetly and calmly. "It's just bears."

"*Just* bears?" Crista cried. "I don't think you understand the situation here, Miss Tish!"

Lindy wrinkled her nose. "You call me 'Miss Tish' when I'm being per...persni...What's that word?"

"Persnickity, little girl!" Crista had to smile in spite of herself.

"Well, I *like* being persnickity," Lindy declared.

"Yeah." Jeff grinned. "Even if you don't know what it means."

The three of them watched for a few more seconds as policemen and circus people scurried about. Crista guessed there were several people scouring the woods for the missing animals. She could hear them all shouting back and forth.

Crista chewed her lip with concern, wondering whether these bears would attack people on horses, but it was plain they weren't in immediate danger. She counted six policemen with guns drawn on the other side of the road, just beyond the line of circus trucks.

The three horses calmed down again and began nipping at some of the new dark green grass by the road. Crista kept pulling up on the reins to keep Betsarama alert. "Guess we won't be going into the woods in the near future," she said. "Unless they catch them."

"That is so cool!" Lindy exclaimed, her freckly face covered all over with excitement and wonder. "Real bears. I've never seen a real bear in the woods."

"These aren't real bears," Jeff interjected. "They're circus bears."

The searchers were in full gear now, with policemen clutching their shotguns as if at any moment one of the bears would come crashing out of the woods and into their laps. Crista knew that three bears loose in the woods was dangerous—real dangerous. Circus bears or not, they still had teeth and claws, and that could do damage.

Lindy's excitement quickly turned to concern. "Do you think they'll shoot them?" she asked.

Suddenly, another roar cracked through the woods. The hair on Crista's neck went straight out. Betsarama clattered forward down the road. Crista pulled her back one more time and cried, "I think we should get out of here."

"But I want to see them!" Lindy yelled.

"How close do we need to get?" Crista asked angrily. "We can see them from a distance."

Now she was nervous. Betsarama's skittishness made her feel as if she might lose control of the horse. That had happened once before when Lindy was riding Lukas, and it led to a crazy gallop through the woods that almost killed Lindy and Crista both.

Suddenly, a third roar slashed the air, and all three horses wheeled. It was not a roar of greeting but of a bear who wanted to fight.

"Hey, you kids, get movin'!" shouted the policeman. "You can't stay here! I'm not telling you again."

"All right, all right!" Jeff called.

They turned the horses to go back. But in a moment there was another pained bawl. This time it sounded like the cry of a trapped animal.

"Over here!" someone was yelling. "Two of them. Up here."

"We'd better go," Crista said nervously.

Jeff grinned. "Let's go up that way—" he pointed down the road, in the opposite direction from home, "and then come back, just to see what's happening."

Policemen and others ran into the woods. Several shotguns clicked and snapped as the officers prepared for action. Jeff gave Thunder a kick and Lindy and Crista followed him down the road. Crista had no problem urging Bets into a gallop.

"Maybe the bears will do some tricks for us," Lindy said as Lukas caught up. She held her cap in one hand and the reins in her other. Lukas's ears were up now as if he had scented something. They surveyed the other trailers as they passed. One looked like a lion cage, though it was covered. There was a monkey truck, too, and many other trailers that were obviously carrying equipment. Most of the trailers had something painted on the side. One featured a trapeze with three figures and said, "The Flying Darlings." Another, in bright red, blue, and orange, pictured several clowns. All the trucks and trailers looked chipped and weather-beaten.

"They're all so old," Lindy stated matter-of-factly. They passed truck after truck with people standing around smoking and talking in hushed groups.

"I think the horses are getting too nervous," Crista finally said. They all slowed down as they neared the end of the line of circus trailers. Crista stopped and turned Betsarama around. Lindy and Jeff followed. As they all started back down the hill, the wind was in their faces now, and a strong smell of bear and hay stung the air.

A second later, they saw Cal, the man in the pith helmet, step onto the road. He was being dragged along by a gigantic bear, the biggest any of the kids had ever seen.

·2·

Two, Not Three

All three of them stopped dead.

"I'm not going any closer," Crista said firmly.

"Oh, come on. It looks okay," Jeff encouraged. 'He's got him on a leash."

Cal braked against the bear, then threw on a muzzle. He shouted and pulled on a choke chain around its neck. "Stop it, Vinnie. Stop!"

The bear stood on its hind legs and pawed the air a moment, as if boxing, then fell back onto all fours. The children watched as the man muzzled the bear, then led him back to the truck. He tied the bear up to the shattered trailer and began talking with a thick-chested bearded man who looked like a genuine pirate.

"They must be Kodiak bears or maybe big brown bears," Jeff said, as they watched Cal strike the bear with a stick to keep him from standing up. The bear appeared to be relatively submissive, not at all defiant, though Crista wondered if he hadn't enjoyed his freedom.

"Might even be a grizzly," Lindy put in. "Grizzlies are mean."

"No way it's a grizzly." Jeff shook his head. "I don't think they can be tamed."

13

"You think he looks tamed?" Crista exclaimed. "I don't think I'm going to run up and give him a kiss."

"Maybe you can blow him one from here," Lindy teased, grinning.

The bear jerked and pulled on the chain.

"We'd better just get by it all now," Crista said. "We have to get Lindy home—it's past four-thirty."

"Yeah, but we have to pass by the bear." Jeff sounded less than sure of himself.

"If we hurry by—trotting—it'll be okay, I think," Crista said. "Just stick as far as you can to the outside. Let's go single file. I'll lead. Lindy, you next, then Jeff. Don't stop. Hear?"

"Got it," Jeff said.

Suddenly, another roar cut the quiet. Cal whipped around, and Crista heard someone say, "They have Val now, too. Two down, one to go." A moment later, a woman stepped out of the woods pulling the second bear by another choke chain.

Crista had slowed Betsarama down to a walk, not wanting to make a commotion when she went by the truck where the first bear was tied.

Turning to the others, Crista whispered, "Be careful now."

"Oh, I'm not scared of a little old bear," Lindy announced. She smiled brightly and Crista shook her head.

"No wisecracks, little girl."

"Aye aye, sir."

The policeman had let some traffic through, but with the appearance of the second bear, everything stopped. Crista watched as the woman led the second bear into the clearing by the road. The woman was young, with blonde hair. "Got her, Cal," she said to

Cal. The bear pulled on the choke chain and was muzzled now. But it looked fierce and angry.

Crista, Lindy, and Jeff waited a moment on the shoulder, unsure of what to do. The woman led the bear over toward the other one.

"Let's wait till they have the bears in the cage," Crista suddenly suggested.

"But that could take hours," Lindy wailed. "And I have to get home."

Crista didn't know whether Lindy really wanted to go or that she just wanted to get a closer look. That would be typical Lindy behavior.

Then the policeman yelled, "You kids, get along now. I'm getting tired of telling you this. This is dangerous business."

"Okay," Crista called back to him. "Just let us pass through."

He waved them on.

Crista patted Betsarama on the neck. Though the horse acted more than skittish, all they had to do was get past this one point, and they'd be home free.

"Okay, let's go for it," she said.

She nudged Betsarama ahead. She could see the bears clearly now. They were both large, with thick silverish hair that glinted in the sunlight. Crista had never noticed anything like that in bears before and wondered what it meant. Several times, the first bear named Vinnie stood on his hind legs and raised his paws in the air, growling. But Cal the trainer acted like this was nothing out of the norm and simply whacked the bear in the shin. It came down on all fours right away.

The woman still held the second bear by the tether. The horses advanced and they were now close to the trailer. Crista's heart thump-thumped in her chest, and her stomach felt as if the butterflies had gone nuts and were fluttering right up to her throat. She knew horses did not see well, but they had to smell the bears. She kept patting Betsarama's neck and head. "Easy girl, easy," she soothed.

The bears sat scratching themselves in a hunch on the other side of the road. It was then that another policeman saw Crista and the others for the first time. He blew his whistle. "You shouldn't be out..." He started running toward them.

Immediately, the second bear stood up and bellowed. She jerked the tether from the woman and lumbered out into the road. Crista froze, pulling Betsarama up with Lindy and Jeff behind her. The policeman stopped in his tracks and stared at the bear in the middle of the street. He slowly drew his pistol.

"No one move," the man named Cal said. "Don't move."

He started walking toward the bear.

That was when it happened. The bear padded across the highway in front of the three horses. Crista blinked, terrified. Betsarama seemed frozen in place. The bear rose up, churned its paws, and bellowed. Crista could feel its hot breath in the cold air. The bear had to be nine feet tall. It looked like a mountain of fur in front of her, all fur and black claws and white teeth.

Just as suddenly, Cal slapped the bear with a big stick and grabbed the choke chain. "Unbelievable, Val," he said. "You know you shouldn't scare people!"

He looked at Crista, still rooted to the saddle and unable to speak. "I'm sorry, miss," Cal apologized. "Seems my bears have developed some bad manners of late." He tipped his hat. The bear sank down and sat on its haunches. The man jerked the chain and the bear began walking back to the truck.

Crista closed her eyes, feeling faint. Behind her, Lindy said, "Wow!"

And Jeff murmured, "Now that was something."

Crista just gave Betsarama a nudge. As if struck by lightning, the big horse leaped into a gallop and couldn't be stopped for half a mile! Lindy and Jeff followed, catching her a minute later. Crista felt in a daze, still half-faint from facing down the bear.

Slowing down, Jeff exclaimed, "That was rad, really rad!"

Jeff's voice brought Crista back to the present. She just shook her head, her heart still in her throat. "I was so scared. I mean, *scared*."

"You didn't act like it," Lindy objected.

"Yeah, you were as cool as a banana," Jeff said.

"A banana?" Crista asked, rolling her eyes.

"Banana split, I mean." Jeff grinned at her. "You okay?"

"Yeah."

As they all walked along, Lindy and Jeff chattered about what a great story Crista's bear experience was. But Crista just kept her eyes on the road, praying that her heart would slow down.

"I heard them say there was one more still in the woods," Lindy said.

"Yeah," Jeff agreed. "Did you hear that, Crista?"

She just shook her head.

Jeff looked at Lindy. "I think Crista had the heebie-jeebies scared out of her."

"Yeah, it was totally cool!"

They all trotted on in silence until Jeff spoke up, "Maybe we could capture him ourselves."

"Yeah, with your slingshot," Lindy replied.

"Right, but I'd have to use bear-sized ammo."

Crista turned around and stared at them. "We are not, I repeat, *not* going into the woods until the other bear is caught."

"Oh, come on, I can protect you," Jeff said.

"With what?"

"My slingshot and my bear-sized ammo."

"Oh, right. And how big is that?" Crista asked, feeling wrung out and tired now.

"Big enough to blow down your door."

"Just try it." She knew Jeff was trying to cheer her up, but her hands were still shaking.

"I think they're cute," Lindy suddenly said, as if hurt by the notion that any one of these bears could be truly dangerous. "I bet that one bear was just trying to do her circus act for Crista."

Crista rolled her eyes with exasperation. "Of course, that must be it. She just wanted to give me my own show."

"Don't get sarcastic." Jeff gave Crista a warning look. "Nothing happened."

"It could've."

"But it didn't."

"It's just that I've never been so scared before."

When they reached the turnoff to the Wilkinses' farm, Crista said, "What if they don't catch the bear in the woods?" She was worried now that she'd never be able to go into the woods again without feeling terrified.

"Then somebody'll be cooking up a mean batch of bear stew for dinner," Jeff joked.

"No way," Lindy protested. "I'm going to find him and make him do his tricks for me, then I'll lead him to the land of the fairies so he'll always be free."

Jeff laughed. "The land of the fairies!" he exclaimed.

"Yeah," Lindy insisted. "Where all your dreams come true."

"You've been reading too many *Where's Waldo?* books, Lindy," Jeff said.

"You don't read them," Lindy replied huffily, trotting by with her nose in the air. "You look at them. And anyway, since you've never been there, don't put it down."

"Oh, and you have!" Jeff laughed even harder.

"Sure," Lindy said. "Every night." She gave Crista a boisterous, "faking-the-guy-out" look, and then kicked Lukas into a faster trot. "First one to the land of the fairies gets one of my mom's cream puff Napoleons!"

"All right!" Jeff yelled and bolted after her on Thunder.

Crista, though, didn't follow. She was still shaking, afraid if she didn't calm down she'd fall off the horse. Half of her worried they wouldn't get the bear, and the other half worried they'd shoot him. She didn't want either to happen.

Still, she thought, maybe Lindy was right. Maybe that bear *had* been doing her circus act. She didn't swipe with her paw at them. Come to think of it, she hadn't really acted like she was going to attack.

Crista let out a long sigh. "Please, God," she prayed. "Let them find the bear and take him home."

A moment later, she remembered Cal's words about sabotage. Was someone really out to do in the bears? To the point of causing a trailer accident?

A moment later, Jeff called from way ahead, "Come on, Crista!"

Regaining her composure, Crista gave Betsarama a pat on the neck. "All right, girl. Can't worry about everything here. Let's show them what you're made of."

Crista gave the horse a little nudge with her heels, and Betsarama leaped forward right into a canter. The wind blew Crista's hair back, and she felt wild and deeply alive for a few seconds. It was the most wonderful feeling on earth. The wind in her face made her eyes tear, but the solid weight of the horse underneath infused her with a deep sense of joy.

·3·

The Bear Facts

That evening as Crista prepared dinner, she opened the old *Encyclopedia Britannica* that her father kept in his little office at the house. She found the entry on bears and discovered a long list of the different types of bears in the world. Then on a hunch she looked up "black bear" and "brown bear." Neither of the bears she'd seen that day were explicitly black or even brown, and she remembered the silver color she'd noticed glinting in the sunlight. She was still unsure of what that meant.

Heating up the stir fry she was making in oil, Crista bent over the book and read everything she could on bears. There was nothing about taming them or their role in zoos or circuses.

Then on a whim she went back into the office and picked up another volume. Her heart almost pounding, she turned to the article on grizzly bears. Right after the name was the word "Silvertip."

Astonished, Crista read on and learned that there were more than eighty different subspecies of grizzly bears, from the big Kodiak and Alaskan brown bears to the more common grizzled bear of the national parks out West. It was the silvered or pale tips of the hair that gave the bear the grizzled effect which she thought matched what she'd seen in the bears that day.

"Boy, real grizzly bears," she said to herself. "That could really mean trouble. No wonder the men had guns."

Swirling the stir fry around, she cut up peppers, onions, and bamboo hearts into the mass. The spicy aroma made her mouth water. She then added meat, and the mixture made her stomach almost turn over. She'd forgotten how hungry she was!

Five minutes later, she heard the front door open and her father stamping his feet on the sill.

"Daddy, that you?"

"Yes, honey! How are you doing?"

He walked into the kitchen and smiled. Her doctor father was tall, with dark hair and a mustache. He had blue eyes, not a bit like Crista's golden eyes which she'd never seen on anyone else except her mother when she was alive. Her mother had died over a year before, killed by a drunk driver.

"I brought you something," her father said.

Crista turned from the stir fry and smiled. "What?"

"A book on photography!" He held it up. "It's called *Getting the Great Shots*, and it has . . ."

Crista rushed over to him, wiping her hands off. "This is just what I need."

"Yeah," he said, his eyes smiling. "It tells you how to look for the right pictures, where to go for what kinds, and all sorts of things. Plus it has some of the great photos of all time, the Pulitzer prize winners and everything. I knew I had to get it the moment I saw it."

Grabbing her father around the neck, Crista kissed him. "Thanks so much, Daddy. I love you."

Her father blushed, suddenly looking shy and humbled. He said nothing more until he took off his coat. "So what's for dinner? It smells good."

"Stir fry. I'm trying something new. Since you gave me this electric wok for Christmas, I've been learning all sorts of new things."

"I know, and trying them out on me."

"Well, you like it, don't you?"

He laughed. "Of course." Walking over to her back at the wok, he gripped her at the shoulders. "I don't know what I'd do without you, honey."

"Me either," Crista said.

"You don't know what you'd do without you, huh?"

"No, without you."

He held her tight a moment, then let go. "I hear there was a quite a commotion up here this afternoon," he remarked. "Something about a circus accident and some loose bears."

"We saw it." Crista told him about all that she had seen up on Route 590 and about the bears, Cal, and the man with the beard. She decided not to mention the confrontation with the big female grizzly. She added, "I wish I had the camera with me."

"Well, don't you be going into those woods till that third bear is captured, all right?"

"Of course, Daddy." She paused and added some soy sauce to the stir fry. "Although I do feel kinda sorry for the bear, being all cooped up in that little cage all the time. The zoo is better than that. And then having to perform with that man Cal whacking him in the legs all the time. It mustn't be much fun."

"I don't know if bears think in terms of fun," Dr. Mayfield said as he walked out of the kitchen toward the living room. "I'm going to do some reading before dinner. Oh, and," he stuck his head around the corner, "don't get thinking that you can bring home that bear like you brought home Rontu and Tigger!" Rontu and Tigger were two dogs Crista had rescued from the wild in the fall. Rontu was an albino Great Dane and Tigger a little Shelty.

"Dad!"

"I mean it, Crista. No going into the woods."

"What about Nadine and Johnny?"

He sighed unhappily.

"I really ought to let them know a bear's loose in the woods," Crista said. "They don't have a TV and chances of them hearing it on the radio are slim."

"All right. You can go by Johnny and Nadine's, but only on horseback and not alone. And you have to go by the road, not by the trail in the woods. Get Jeff to go with you."

"Thanks, Dad."

After dinner, Crista sat in the living room with her dad ensconced in his Lazyboy chair reading medical journals. She thumbed through the photography book, examining the pictures, oohing and aahing over several wonderful prizewinning photos of kids from different lands in full costume dress. She didn't read much of the text, knowing she could do that later. It was perfect.

She glanced up several times at her father and, catching him watching her, flashed him a happy smile. She liked it when her dad acted happy. Not that he didn't act that way that much, but it was good to see him in a joyous mood. She knew he liked to give her gifts. With Mom gone, Crista realized that in some ways she was all he had anymore. More than once, she

had resolved to give him as little trouble as she could—
short of not doing something she needed to do, like get
a picture of the circus bear in the wild. But she wasn't
going to jeopardize herself or Jeff or Lindy or anyone
else to do that. She simply hoped she could get a
decent shot sometime in the next few days, maybe
after they found the bear. She resolved to keep a lookout.

As she thought about the bears, though, the image
of that huge grizzly in front of her and Betsarama
crackled into her memory. She could see the whole
thing. Even the scent came back. She began to shiver.

Immediately, she heard her father's voice. "Crista!
Crista! Are you okay?"

She blinked and turned to look at her father.

"You looked like you'd zonked out or something."

Crista breathed in deeply, then sighed. "Just thinking about those bears." With a sudden rush, her whole
frame quaked and tears came into her eyes. Her father
got up and grasped her. "What's the matter, honey?"

The whole story finally spilled out. Her father
peered into her eyes gravely. "You've just had a panic-
reaction," he said. "It happens to some people. They
don't really get scared until long after the horrible
thing has happened. You'll be okay."

He hugged her and she said, "I think I'm going to
get to bed early tonight." She kissed her dad then
walked down the hall to her room and changed into
her pajamas. By her bed Crista prayed, "Lord, please
help the bear trainer Cal to find his bear, and don't let
anyone get hurt. Thanks."

* * *

The next morning, Crista picked up the paper left out front and immediately read the headline: "Circus Truck Loses Rear Axle; Bear Escapes."

The article was written by a reporter named Steve Leonard from the local branch of the *Bucks County Times*, and it told how missing lug nuts had caused the trailer to fall over, releasing the three bears. Two were readily captured, but a third had disappeared quickly into the woods and no one had seen him since the escape. The bears' names were Vinnie, Val, and Vic, as the kids had heard, and were part of a special act in The Halloran Brothers Mini-Circus Troupe, a little circus which went through Pennsylvania and the eastern United States, bringing their show to the small towns and villages. They normally stayed a week in one place. Crista remembered seeing a circus the year before at one of the state fairs and it had been fun. But she hadn't seen the bear act.

The reporter had interviewed Cal Turner for the article. His stage name was "Daring Dan," but everyone called him Cal as Crista and Jeff had heard the previous day on the road. He said that a bear like Vic could make ten or twenty miles a day, foraging for bugs, fish, rabbits, and whatever else it could scare up to eat. But normally, a grizzly bear would find a cave or hollow and create a home base, then go out from there. However, Turner said, "I don't know how well Vic will fare in the wild. I've had him since he was born, like the two others. So he's never really lived in the woods."

The article didn't mention Crista's escapade. She was glad of that. She didn't want to talk about it any more than she had to.

* * *

That day after school, Crista and Jeff decided to ride over to Nadine and Johnny's and warn them about the bear. After saddling up at the Wilkinses' farm, they stopped at Lindy's, but she was not home. "She's probably at her parents' restaurant," Crista said as they remounted the horses.

"Maybe next time," Jeff replied. "She'll be upset, though."

They trotted down the road to the turnoff where they headed in toward Nadine and Johnny's. For early April weather, it was still cold. They both wore parkas, jeans, boots, and gloves. Crista wore a little multicolored tam that had once been her mother's on her head.

Nadine and Johnny Semms lived in the nook between two mountains. Nadine had given birth to twins that winter during a terrible snowstorm. The birth made all the headlines because Crista herself had saved the day by running through the woods to get help.

Crista had met Nadine the previous summer on one of her many trips through the woods as she collected flowers and drew pictures in charcoal and watercolor of local trees, shrubs, and rocks. She had helped Nadine and Johnny many times over the past few months, babysitting frequently, and even raising some money to help with the babies' care.

There were two ways to the rustic cabin which sat by a stream in the valley between Moonlight Mountain and the next mountain over. One was the trail across the road from where Crista's cabin was. It led up past the Love Tree, as Crista called it, and then cut west to the little cabin that Johnny had bought from his uncle during the summer. It was a good mile through the woods that way, and it was very close to where the grizzly named Vic had escaped. That way would be especially dangerous. Both Crista and Jeff had listened on the radio for any news of a capture, but no one had yet found the bear.

The other way went by the back dirt roads that led to the dump and other cabins and farms on the back side of the mountain. That route was probably safer. The bear, if it was smart, would not hang around where humans lived.

Cal Turner, however, had said in the newspaper that Vic would not know how to defend himself effectively in the wild. Though most creatures would be afraid of him, he would not be an adept hunter. Chances were that he'd hang around houses and places where he could easily find garbage.

"Like the dump," Jeff said as he and Crista discussed it riding down the trail toward the Semms' house. It was all part of the reason Crista wanted to warn Nadine and Johnny.

"I bet the bear's at the dump all the time!" Crista exclaimed.

"But wouldn't that make it easy for him to be captured?" Jeff asked.

Crista wrinkled her brow with thought. "Yeah, I guess the bear's smarter than that. And don't bears sleep during the day and go out at night?"

"That's owls," Jeff corrected.

"And raccoons, too. But I think some bears do sleep during the day."

"Not big bears like that. They don't see real well, so at night it would be even worse for them."

Jeff clucked to Thunder as he ducked under branches hanging out over the road. "Watch out for that limb there," he said, turning to Crista. "Looks like someone broke it recently." A limb hung lower than usual and both Jeff and Crista led their horses around it.

"I bet a bear that's been in a circus is real smart," Jeff commented.

"Why?" Crista asked. "Just because he can do tricks? Street smarts and woods smarts are two different things."

"Yeah, I guess." Jeff grinned. "You're pretty smart yourself, Crista, old babe, old gal."

Crista gave him a wry frown. "I'm *not* old. And I'm *not* a babe."

"In my book you are."

Blushing, Crista gave Betsarama a little kick. "I think I better get away from you or next thing you know we'll be getting married."

"No way!" Jeff called as he lagged behind, then gave Thunder a rip in the ribs so that the big black horse shot forward and caught up to Crista. "I'm never getting married. But I'm going to have millions and millions of babes. One in every city."

"Dream on!"

"Really. Girls are going to love me cause I'm so handsome and such a hero."

Crista laughed. "Spare me the details."

"You know what a great guy I am. So you shouldn't be laughing."

Crista turned around in the saddle and stopped Betsarama. "You know, if we weren't friends, I'd probably think you were the most stuck-up kid on the block!"

Jeff grinned. Crista knew he liked razzing her like this. Neither of them had ever indicated the least romantic interest in anyone, let alone each other. But every now and then Jeff got on a kick about how handsome he was and how all the beautiful women would be lining up to go out with him and shoot his slingshot. It always made her laugh. He was such a dodo about his slingshot sometimes, as if the whole world revolved around boys shooting BBs up in the air!

"Hey, look," Jeff said as they came around a bend and spotted Nadine in the yard with the twins on their little bouncy swings. They were each wearing snowsuits, a powder-blue one for Johnny Junior and a pink one for Fairlight. Nadine had found the outfits at a local secondhand store.

"Geddup, Bets." The horse sprang into a canter with Crista whooping and reining around the curve into the yard.

"Hey! Hey! Hey!" Nadine was shouting as Jeff caught up. "Watch out for the little ones!"

"I'm watching," Crista cried, as she pulled Betsarama to a stop, then nearly leaped off the horse into Nadine's arms. "Do you know about the bear?"

Nadine laughed. "Oh, that old circus bear. Johnny's going to shoot him and skin him!"

"No!"

"Right, no!" Nadine's deep crystal-blue eyes shone with humor. "But he is going to join the search crew today. They were hoping to find the bear around the dump, but no one's seen hide nor hair of him at all. Least that's what I know."

"Aren't you scared for the kids?" Crista asked, looking at the twins. Both were towheads, hair blonder than Nadine's, whose long tresses were nearly white.

"Nah," Nadine answered, stooping down and giving Johnny Junior a little kiss on the forehead. Both tots bounced in their springy seats and gurgled. They were each only four months old, but Nadine said she had them on the "fast track to success," whatever that was. "Johnny's got his rifle and I know how to shoot, too, since he taught me during the winter. And they say this bear is fairly tame, so I'm not too worried." She pointed to a rifle leaning up against the side of the house, and next to it was a shotgun. For the first time, Crista noticed both guns.

"Well, that sure beats everything," Crista said. "And here Jeff and I thought we were going to save you!"

Jeff stepped off Thunder behind Crista and Nadine and tied the reins around the post in front of the little cabin. "Yeah, we thought we'd give you a good scare."

"Not a scare!" Crista exclaimed. "Good grief, we're not trying to scare anyone."

"Don't get upset, Crista. I understand," Nadine said. "As for you, Jeff Pallaci, I have a real bone to pick with you."

"What's that?" Jeff asked.

"Last time you babysat with Crista, you changed Johnny Junior without powdering him and he had the worst case of diaper rash..."

"I didn't change him, Crista did!"

"No I didn't, dearie." Crista smiled sweetly. "You insisted. Remember?"

"All right, all right," Jeff replied. "What—I never get to change the little pooper-dooper again? That's okay with me."

Nadine laughed. "Well, you aren't until you've had some remedial work in changing diapers! But just that you changed him was incredible enough, Jeffy, my boy. So I'm not going to complain."

Nadine picked up little Fairlight and started to take her inside. "Well, come on, I've got a pie baking in the oven. You can each have a bite, if you help me get the kids in and bring in some wood."

"Sure," Jeff said, immediately heading around the side of the house to the woodpile. Crista jostled Johnny Junior out of his seat and pulled him into her arms, then went inside behind Nadine.

After situating Fairlight in the playpen, Nadine went to the oven and turned off the gas. "Johnny's finally got this stove working right for once. Scares me to death half the time."

Crista set Johnny Junior down next to his sister. He gurgled approval and stayed on his back, legs and arms weaving back and forth.

"Come on, let's get that wood." Nadine led Crista back out onto the porch. Jeff was just dropping his second armful of split wood into the bin outside the front door.

"A few more and we'll be done," Nadine said.

"Aw, you go in with the little ones," Jeff said, as he headed back to the woodpile. "I'll finish this. I need the exercise, to build up my muscles."

"I didn't know you had them." Nadine rolled her eyes at Crista. "Is it a new addition?"

"Give me a break, or I'll eat your whole pie," Jeff called over his shoulder.

Suddenly there was a loud pop inside. Everyone turned. Through the window it looked like the whole kitchen area was in flames.

"The oven exploded!" Nadine yelled.

·4·

A Strange Visitor in the Trees

Everyone ran for the house. "Get the children!" Crista screamed.

As Nadine and Crista grabbed Johnny Junior and Fairlight out of the playpen, Jeff doused a towel in a bowl of water and beat at the flames. It was only a small gas fire, contained above the stove on one of the burners.

"It's the darn pilot light and that left burner," Nadine said, panting as she and Crista watched Jeff put out the flames. "It goes out sometimes when you turn off the burners. Then there's a slight gas buildup and if things are still hot, it can ignite."

"Well, that's what must have happened," Jeff said as he whapped the last of the flickering flames with the towel. In less than a minute, the whole episode was over.

"Wow!" Crista was still kind of shaky. "What if that had happened when no one was here? It could have burned down your cabin."

"I know." Nadine bit her lower lip in concern. "That's why I'm going to have Johnny call in a regular repairman. We really should get a new stove, but Johnny's barely making enough to keep food on the table. I wish it could be repaired properly. Johnny's handy, but he doesn't know everything."

34

Wiping his hands off, Jeff said, "I'd better relight the pilot light so that doesn't happen again."

"Do you know how to do it?" Crista asked.

"Sure. My grandma's is the same kind. We had a fire like this once. It's a problem with old gas stoves, I bet. If the pilot light goes out, that little dribble of gas can build up. And then, kaboom."

Crista frowned at him. "Don't say that!"

"You're telling me," Nadine sighed. "All right, light the pilot light and let's get this cleaned up. Looks like my pie is done for."

"Oh, I like it a little black," Jeff said, grinning.

They set the babies back in the playpen. Neither of them acted as if anything strange had happened. Both just burbled and smiled away. "Fairlight's more smiley than Johnny Junior," Crista said.

"Yeah, I know. Johnny says it's gas."

Crista laughed. "Could be."

As Crista played with the children and Jeff relit the pilot light, Nadine bustled about collecting toys and placing them into the playpen. "They can't play much yet, but I like to think they'll try if I spread everything out," Nadine said to Crista as she dropped in a plastic block in which all different shapes were pushed through appropriate holes to the inside. "They're both going to be geniuses, so I figure starting them early is never too early."

She finished what she was doing and sat down. "I'm glad you were here when that happened. I sure don't need any more bad news than I've already got."

"Bad news?" Crista asked.

"Yeah, we just found out on Saturday. Johnny Junior has a hernia."

"A hernia!" Jeff exclaimed with obvious surprise. "What's he lifting?"

"Nothing," Nadine said. "It was congenital. Apparently he was born with it and we didn't know. The doctors just diagnosed it. Johnny Junior needs an operation and it's going to cost plenty. You know, Johnny Senior's not permanent at the station yet and doesn't have any health insurance. So we are in a real pickle."

"How much will it cost?" Crista asked as she sat Fairlight on her lap and let the tiny girl grip her index finger. Now she was worried. Nadine and Johnny were very poor but they didn't like to take handouts.

"Several thousand dollars I expect," Nadine said.

As Crista and Jeff's faces lit with concern, Nadine smiled sadly. "Yeah, that's what I said. I guess I'm just gonna have to send Johnny Junior back where he came from."

Crista frowned. "I don't think that's going to happen."

"Yeah, just trying to make light of a bad situation," Nadine replied. "We'll figure it out somehow."

Everyone was silent for a moment, and Jeff walked over to the door to look outside. He put his hands in his pockets and rocked back and forth on his boots just like Johnny Senior himself did. Nadine said nothing but she pointed to him. Crista nodded and whispered, "He picks up a lot of things like that. But mainly he wants to be a champion slingshot shooter!"

"What?!" Jeff said, swinging around.

"Just girl talk," Nadine said, stifling a grin.

Jeff clopped back in and sat down. "I do believe I'll try a piece of that pie, burned or not. We'll just call it Cajun pie."

"Cajun?" Crista asked.

"Yeah, you know—down in New Orleans. Hot. Spicy. Blackened."

"Oh, yeah. I've tried to do that several times."

"It's good," Jeff added. "I like it anyway. So bring it on."

Nadine set a piece of the blackened pie in front of him when suddenly both horses whinnied with obvious fear.

"Something's up," Jeff said.

Nadine ran over to the window and looked out. Both horses were backing and moving around with anxiety. "I'm going to take a look," she said. "There's something out there. I hope it's not that bear."

Jeff hurried to the door and Nadine stooped to pick up Johnny Junior. She and Crista went to the door with the children in their arms. Jeff ran outside to the horses. "Easy, Thunder. What is it? Hear something, Betsarama?"

"You don't think it could be the bear—around here?" Crista tried to stay calm.

"I don't know," Nadine said ominously. "Think it would come this close, with people around?"

"It's pretty tame, they said," Crista commented.

Jeff took out his slingshot and put a little steel ball into the pouch.

"Don't shoot at him," Crista said immediately. "You don't want to make him mad. And the book I read said you have to be real careful not to surprise them. Like when you're going through the woods, you should whistle and talk, so they hear you coming and aren't surprised. That's when they attack."

"Let me get the shotgun," Nadine said. "A slingshot won't do anything to something really dangerous."

She handed Johnny Junior to Crista and then went around the side of the house to retrieve the shotgun. She came back with Johnny's pump-action twelve gauge. It was an older model, but the stock and wooden pump were shiny with polish. Nadine fed in three shells.

Jeff asked, "Do you think it could be the bear?"

"I don't know," Nadine answered. "But I'm not waiting to find out. I'm going to take a look around."

The horses continued nickering and jostling back and forth. Their frenzy had died some, but they were still obviously afraid.

"I'll go with you," Jeff said. "You want me to take the gun?"

"I know how to use it," Nadine said. "And you need to stay here to keep the horses calm." She stepped off the porch and turned to Jeff again. "If it is the bear and he comes after the horses, set them loose. They'll have a better chance if they can run."

Jeff just nodded silently, his eyes wide.

Crista went back into the house and watched through the window as Nadine walked toward the woods to her left. It was a bit dark under the fronds of the just-budding trees and a bear could easily hide among them and not be seen. Crista's heart beat loud and hard as she waited. She hoped it wasn't the bear. She didn't want it to get shot, and she didn't want Nadine to get hurt, either. Or Jeff. Or herself. After what had happened the day before, she knew she didn't want to face down some hungry bear.

Nadine advanced slowly. She had the gun out straight, ready to shoot if she needed to.

Then off to their right, there was a rustle.

Nadine whipped around and stood her ground. There was a swishing of leaves and branches deeper in the woods. Something was running.

Crista's heart banged inside her chest. She held onto the twins tightly and waited. What was Nadine doing—trying to get mauled?

"It could be deer," Nadine said, still peering at the woods.

Crista called to her, "Come back over here! I don't like this."

"Yeah," Jeff said. "We'll be much safer in the house."

"But I've got to know what it is," Nadine insisted. She raised the gun and pointed at the top of the trees and fired. *Blam.* The leaves and trees rattled with the buckshot. Birds flew up in a twittering of voices. Squirrels skittered around in the forest.

Then all was quiet. Nadine suddenly appeared frail and pale in the stark light. She certainly looked nothing like a shotgun-wielding grizzly-shooter!

They waited in silence for another minute.

Jeff said, "I think it's gone."

"Yeah, I think you're right," Nadine agreed. "And I don't like standing here with only two shells in the gun. A bear can get up to thirty miles an hour, I think."

Crista called again, "Would you all please get back in the house!"

"Yeah," Nadine said. "I don't know what it was, but it's gone now. The horses have calmed down."

Crista called one more time. Nadine backed up and Jeff began to untie the horses. "I'll tether them a little closer to the front door." He caressed Thunder's neck. "What was it, boy? A bear? Was it a bear you smelled?"

The horse snorted and stamped its foot, glancing apprehensively toward the woods. Jeff began walking them around. Nadine backed all the way up to the cabin and took her post on the porch. Everyone was still nervous—first a fire and now an unknown visitor.

Crista's heart was still pounding and her mouth felt dry. "It might have been a dump dog," she offered, joining Nadine on the porch. A whole pack of lost and rejected dogs cruised around the mountain area, staying close to the dump where they could find food. Rontu and Tigger, Crista's two dogs, had once been dump dogs before she rescued them. "I wish my dogs were here," she said quietly.

"Yeah," Nadine said, ejecting the two rounds from the shotgun and putting them into her pocket. She leaned the shotgun against the log wall. "Next time bring Rontu and Tigger with you. We need some watchdogs around here, actually. I wouldn't mind collecting one of those dump mutts myself and taming him."

"You really ought to have one," Crista added.

"Let's go inside. I don't think it's coming back."

"Let's hope so."

A few minutes later, Jeff walked in. He had retied the horses outside. Flecks of black pie crust stuck on his lips and chin, and he looked like Little Jack Horner for a moment, except this wasn't plum pie. Crista and Nadine laughed and the tension was broken at last.

"Maybe we're just all spooked," Nadine said. "It might have been a very large squirrel."

Crista set down Johnny Junior in the playpen. Nadine put the shotgun and shells away on the rack hanging over the fireplace. Everything in the cabin looked normal again. Crista felt relieved.

"And to think I was going to ask you to babysit this Friday night."

"Well, why not?" Crista asked.

"I don't know," Nadine said. "Not with all this happening."

"Oh, Jeff'll come with me, won't you, Jeff?"

"Sure," Jeff said, digging into another piece of pie. "And if you bake another pie that isn't Cajun brand, I'll do double duty as protector and handsome boy in the yard."

Both girls chuckled. "Jeff is back to normal," Nadine observed.

Crista said, "That's for sure."

But Nadine kept looking fearfully out the front door, and Crista listened between the thumps of her heart.

As she and Jeff rode home later on, Crista said, "I've got to help Nadine with Johnny Junior's operation. He has to have it."

"But how can you help?" Jeff asked.

"I don't know. Maybe I can sell some paintings."

"But you've never made much money from that. And Nadine said it would be thousands of dollars."

"I can't just sit back and let him suffer."

"Yeah, I know. And there's that stove, too."

Crista ducked to avoid a hanging branch. "It seems like things never get better, you know?"

"Yeah," Jeff agreed. "And now we have more than our share."

"I know." Crista sank back into her thoughts as Betsarama trotted happily along. A hernia was serious. She knew that. And she knew it wasn't something that her father normally performed surgery for, so he couldn't help.

·5·

The Bear Trainer

As they trotted down the road, Jeff pointed out a truck parked up ahead. It was black and white, covered with zebra stripes. "Must be one of the circus trucks," he said.

Crista pulled up Betsarama. "What do you think they're doing?"

Jeff stopped Thunder beside her. "Maybe we should let the horses graze for a second. See if someone shows up."

Crista felt especially nervous on the road, with the possibility of the bear being around. But if the truck was from the circus, someone had to be nearby. She would like to hear their side of this whole mess. She let Betsarama lean down and bite at small tufts of grass growing by the roadside. It was still cold, but all the snow was gone.

The two of them waited in silence, listening to sounds in the woods, half expecting something to jump out and grab them. Then Crista heard a leafy shuffling sound in the woods.

"Someone's coming," she whispered. She strained to see who it was. Jeff stood up in the stirrups, peering just as attentively.

A man appeared. It was the man with the pith helmet, Cal Turner, except this time he wore a brown hunter's cap. He was old and skinny, but he walked confidently, solemnly, staring at the ground and banging a staff against trees and parting bushes.

Jeff whispered, "He must be searching for tracks or something. Is he alone?"

"I think so. He doesn't act like he's with anyone."

At the sound, the man looked up. He grinned broadly and walked toward them. "Hello," he greeted. "So you're back. You horseback riding out here? I should have thought yesterday's scare was enough to keep you away from the woods forever."

"Yeah," Crista said, offering nothing else. She was very nervous.

"Do you know about my Victor?"

"The bear?" Crista asked. She glanced at Jeff and they both dismounted.

"My grizzly. The greatest show bear on earth. Do you know that he lets me sit on his shoulders? Just like Grizzly Adams of old. You know about Grizzly Adams?"

They both shook their heads.

"A great old animal trainer, hunter, and showman." The man walked up to them and held out his hand. "I'm Cal Turner, known better as Daring Dan of the Halloran Brothers Circus."

Crista gave his hand a quick shake and so did Jeff, then they introduced themselves. "We've been reading about the escaped bear—I mean, grizzly—in the newspaper."

Cal's eyes looked like they were watering. "If I lose him, I lose everything. I raised him from a cub. His mother was our first trick bear, and she and one of my males—Samson—mated. I raised him. Fed him with a bottle. Like my own son."

Swallowing, Crista watched the old man's eyes. They were a deep emerald green, sharp and craggy. He had thick, hairy eyebrows that needed plucking or shaving a bit, and there were hairs poking out of his ears and nose. His nose was majestic, a long wide curve like some prehistoric bird beak. His chin was cleft, and he sported a long handlebar mustache. He looked like some old cowboy out of the West, and except for the hunter's cap, he would have been a fearsome sight. But Crista could tell he was very gentle.

"I've been out here all day and night. Vic cannot survive like this. He's a tame bear. Wouldn't hurt anyone. And that sheriff—ugh! He hasn't a clue as to how to track a bear. I don't know what to do." The old man seemed to be half talking to himself and not to Crista and Jeff. He had a far-off, pained look in his eyes.

"You know, a bear like that, they look fierce and formidable—that's the whole catch of the thing and the show. But he's gentle. Played with my sheepdog, Sylvester, every day till Ves died about a year ago. Vic went into mourning, and so did..."

Suddenly, he looked at Crista and Jeff, as if noticing them for the first time.

"Oh, I shouldn't go on like this. I'm just an old man, and you are two young kids. But if you see him, if you give me information that leads to his cap—no, I mean, his return to safety, I'll give a $500 reward." He sighed and looked toward the woods. "I don't know why I'm doing it. The circus is on the skids, just about broke. Boss doesn't even half care if the bear disappears for good. I don't know what to do. And the whole thing looks like sabotage to me." He looked Crista deeply in the eyes. "I guess you don't understand. But I love that bear. Like my own son. I even named him my favorite name in all the world: Victor. That's the name of my own first son, who died in the war. Vietnam." He turned away and poked at the weeds.

"What can we do?" Crista asked.

"Look for tracks. Look for patties. Look in places where there's food. I know he's desperate by now. Thinking about freedom and then his life with the circus. Confused. Real confused. I know that feeling." He looked at Crista again. "I'm just rambling. But you get my drift. Can you help? Can you help an old man find his best friend in all the world?"

He looked at Jeff and Crista as if they were doctors or senators or the president and his chief aide. He blinked at the sunlight, then shook his head. "I'm not even making sense. I'm driven to distraction. I don't know what I'm saying and thinking anymore. You'll have to excuse me."

He turned around and walked with a slightly rickety gait back toward the truck. Crista felt for him. He was an old man. Alone. All he had was the circus and his bears. Suddenly, she called after him. "Mr. Turner! Mr. Turner!"

The old man turned around and peered at her just under the rim of the hat. "Yes, miss?"

"I'll help. And so will Jeff. We'll keep a lookout. I promise." Crista suddenly thought of what had happened down at Nadine's. She told Mr. Turner about it.

"Could be, could be," he said. "I'll check it out. You say they're down the road?"

"Yes. At the end."

"All right." He smiled. "Thank you. From the bottom of my heart, thank you. I need all the help I can get."

He turned again and walked, slightly stooped, over to the truck. He started it and roared away.

"He's real old," Jeff said suddenly.

"Yeah, he probably knows this could be his last year in the circus," Crista said. Her lips trembled and her eyes burned. "I feel so bad for him."

"Yeah. He talked like that bear was human."

"Maybe he almost is," Crista said. She started to mount Betsarama, but then turned to Jeff. "Did you hear him say sabotage?"

"Yeah!"

"The same thing he was saying when we first saw the wreck."

"I know," Jeff said. He mounted Thunder.

"Then maybe we can help find out who did it."

Jeff scrunched up his lips with a questioning look. "But how can we help?"

"I think the first thing is to talk to that reporter, Steve Leonard."

"Good idea."

Crista threw her leg over Betsarama's back and gave her a kick. They headed up the road. Her throat was tight as she thought about Nadine, Johnny Junior, and now the bear and Mr. Turner. For a moment she wondered why the world was so full of problems, and then she prayed that these were three that would soon get solved.

·6·

The Newspaper

The next day school was closed for teachers' meetings so Crista decided to call the paper, talk to Steve Leonard, and let him know that the bear might have been in their neighborhood. She also wanted to find out about the sabotage issue. Was anyone checking it out?

When she called, Mr. Leonard decided to come out to the house. There, Crista and Jeff told the story. They also told him about Johnny Junior.

After getting it all down, Mr. Leonard said, "Yeah, well you don't know what else went on last night. Wait till you see tomorrow's paper."

"What?" they both said.

Mr. Leonard opened his notebook and took out a copy of an article obviously made on a fax machine. The headline about the bear said, "Bear Mauls Man at Dump." Crista and Jeff were in shock.

"But he couldn't have!" Crista cried. "He's supposed to be tame."

"Not by this story," the reporter replied. "A Mr. Landesman was at the dump leaving off some garbage when the bear ran up and took a swipe at him, right across the face. He knocked the man down and bit him

47

in the chest, then ran off. If it was the same bear—and what else could it have been?—then he must be going by your friend's cabin in the woods looking for food."

Crista quickly scanned the article. "Maybe the bear was just scared and in his fright he took a swipe at the man."

"Doesn't matter," Mr. Leonard said. "Sheriff now says the bear has to be destroyed. The circus people are protesting, of course, but it's out of their control. Sheriff's got the whole department up on the mountain this morning searching everywhere with orders to shoot on sight. Everyone's looking for that bear now!"

"But what about us?" Jeff objected. "He didn't do anything, just hid in the woods. And what about Mr. Turner? He rides on the bear's back!"

"And what about when the other bear ran out in the road?" Crista said angrily. "She didn't even swipe at us. My friend Lindy thinks she was doing a circus trick." Crista was definitely over the scare from that episode. As she spoke, her father walked into the living room and sat down.

It was as if the reporter didn't hear a thing. "You don't really know that," he said. "And the free bear mauled the man. That's enough for me!"

"Who was this man at the dump anyway?" Crista wanted to know. "How do you know he was really mauled?"

"He was bandaged up when I saw him. Looked pretty bad to me."

"Is he a resident, though?" Dr. Mayfield suddenly asked.

"Only got his name," Mr. Leonard said, looking irritated. "What—you don't think he's telling the truth?"

Jeff and Crista looked at Dr. Mayfield. What did he mean? Crista said, "What are you thinking, Daddy? How would it matter if he was a resident or not, or just one of the summer people up here early for some reason?"

Dr. Mayfield cleared his throat. "From what Mr. Turner says, it doesn't make a lot of sense. Why would the bear just charge this man without provocation? And where did he go to get medical treatment? Did you interview the doctors about his wounds? Seems to me there are a lot of opinions flying about around here, and no one's getting the real facts."

"The story was not made up," Mr. Leonard said defensively. "How do I know *your* story wasn't made up?"

"Why would we make it up?" Crista said, now defensive herself.

"You tell me!" Mr. Leonard stood up. "This guy seemed believable."

"Did you see the actual stitches?" Dr. Mayfield asked.

There was a pause. "Well, no."

"So you don't know if he didn't just dress himself up to look like it."

"But why would he do that?"

"You tell me. You're the investigative reporter. They've been talking about sabotage here. That should be something to go on."

Mr. Leonard swallowed and looked from Crista to Jeff to Dr. Mayfield. He gathered up his notes. "Well, I can't guarantee this'll get into the paper. But I'll do what I can. Meanwhile, I'm going to recheck this Mr. Landesman. I admit I didn't get an address from him. Guess I was a little too excited. But he did look in pretty bad condition to me. I haven't been doing this real long."

"Did you get his license plate?" Dr. Mayfield asked.

"Uh, yeah, actually I did," Mr. Leonard stammered, now obviously embarrassed. "In fact, they were Maryland plates."

"He could still be a resident," Dr. Mayfield said. "But check it out. Find out who this Landesman is. That might be the key to the whole affair."

"And would you tell us when you find out?" Crista asked.

The reporter looked even more embarrassed, but then he brightened. "Look, you want to come down with me to the office? Maybe you can help."

Crista looked at her father, and he smiled, shrugged, and nodded.

"Yeah," she said. "Let's do it. We've got all day."

As they all climbed into Steve Leonard's car, the reporter confessed to Crista and Jeff, "This is my first big story. I mean, I was just a copy editor until this week when they let me loose. I don't really know what I'm doing. I'm sorry I argued with you."

"It's okay," Crista said. "We're not experts either, even if sometimes we act like it."

"And the truth is," Jeff added, "if you don't know what you're doing, we hardly know what planet we're on."

Steve smiled. "Your dad's pretty smart."

"Just like a doctor to ask those questions, that's all," Crista replied.

Turning onto the highway, everyone immediately spotted the line of cars and trucks, police vehicles and men standing around, most of them with guns. Steve whistled. "They're really out for blood now. We'd better check this all out as fast as we can."

"Yeah, because they're gonna kill Vic, sure as shootin'," Jeff said. "No matter what Mr. Turner says. That's probably why he was so depressed yesterday."

They passed the line of cars, just in time to see the men move into the woods. Crista didn't see Johnny Semms there, but Nadine had said he might be one of them. If the bear was out there, he wouldn't escape this time. Crista tried to put the thought out of her mind. She only hoped these men weren't all trigger-happy and determined to bag their first bear.

Jeff peered down at Steve's notes in the notebook, and then he and Crista read the whole story of the mauling as the reporter drove into town. There was a picture of the mauled man on the reverse side. He looked like a wounded person in the middle of a war. The whole left side of his face was covered in gauze.

"Did you interview him in the hospital?" Crista said. "This picture looks like it's outside."

"No, he wasn't in the hospital at the time. He just came down to the office last night late."

"That's weird," Crista said. "You'd think he'd be in the hospital for a few days at least."

"I never thought of that," Steve admitted. "Man, I feel like a real idiot."

"Hey, it's okay. How old are you anyway?" Jeff asked. Crista could tell he liked the man now, despite his poor first impression.

"Twenty-two. Graduated just last May. From Scranton."

"So you're really new at this, huh?"

"Yeah. I told you, this is my first big story."

Crista continued reading the article until she finished. It was well written in terms of style, very dramatic. But there was so little content and no address, no place where Landesman could be reached.

At the little office on Main Street, Steve unlocked the door and led them in. There were only two desks, both strewn with papers and disorganized. "This is just a satellite office," the young reporter explained. "The main office is in Honesdale."

He sat down at the desk. He pointed to the other one and motioned to Jeff and Crista to sit down in the two chairs around it. "We'll start with the license plate number. I have a friend at the police station. I'll give him a call, see if he can tell us who the registered owner of the car is." He dialed the number and talked for a few minutes to his friend, then set the phone down. "Gotta wait now. A lot of reporting, whether you know it or not, is waiting. I found that out."

"Doesn't it get boring?" Jeff said, putting his feet up on the desk and making himself comfortable.

"Hey, that's what I do." Steve grinned. Then he said, "I guess it's no more boring than anything else. You live for a story like this one. And here I've been on it for three days and I've already got one. Most of the time you're trying to rustle up features on local citizens, good deeds, that kind of thing. There's an award every year for some of the best stories, and then of course, there's always the possibility of winning the Pulitzer prize. That's every reporter's dream."

Steve poured himself a cup of coffee and offered one to Crista and Jeff, but neither wanted it. They didn't drink coffee, though Crista had tasted her father's on occasion.

"I could go for a Coke, though," Jeff said.

"Sure. We have them." Steve went back to a little refrigerator. "It costs fifty cents, but I'll pay for you this time. You want one, too, Crista?"

"No, thanks." Crista gazed around the office. It was just a storefront with the name of the paper written across the front glass. People passed by with packages or on their way to other stores. No one paid much attention to the three of them as they sat talking in the office.

In the middle of a sentence, the phone rang.

"Steve Leonard," he said as he picked it up, then nodded to the two kids, mouthing, "It's the police station."

"Yeah . . . yeah . . . let me write that down. Yeah. Okay, thanks!"

Steve looked up at them. "Well, he is from Maryland. And he is just passing through. And his name isn't Landesman, it's Jon Larby. But guess what else?"

"What?"

"He works for the circus."

· 7 ·

Lessons

The next day after school, there had still been no news of the capture of the bear and the hunt had become more frantic. The newspapers said the circus people were accusing the police of being too pushy, and the police were saying the circus people didn't know how to do a manhunt let alone a bear hunt. Crista worried about what they'd do to the bear. But she hoped Steve Leonard found something on Larby. So far, no one but Steve seemed concerned about the sabotage part of the case. Everyone was intent on finding the bear.

When she called Steve's office, though, there was only the answering machine. She left a message, but she knew she would probably go crazy sitting around waiting for Steve to call her back. She decided to go over to Nadine's so they could work on the photography lessons. At least that would take her mind off things for awhile.

Nadine showed Crista first how the focus worked on the camera. It was an old Nikkormat that Crista's mother had owned and used when she worked as a "stringer" for a newspaper during her years before marriage. Just recently Crista's father had given it to her. "Your mother loved this old camera," he had told

Crista. "And she'd be glad to know it's being put to good use." It had been a happy and sad moment for both Crista and her dad.

Nadine held the camera and made several adjustments. "You wait until the little lever in the box inside the viewfinder is right in the middle. You have to move around your f-stop—that controls aperture—and also the shutter speed to get it right." Nadine explained how aperture—the amount of light let into the camera through the diaphragm of the lens—worked with the shutter that opened when Crista pushed the button. Aperture and shutter speed worked together to produce an image on the film. In that instant when the shutter opened and closed, an image was printed on the face of the film. That created the negative which could be turned into a real picture.

"Then all you have to do is focus, and presto, you've got a picture." Nadine put the camera into Crista's hands and she looked through the viewfinder—the part of the camera which frames the picture to be taken.

"I see the lever, yeah," said Crista. "It's way down."

"To bring it up, shift around these two rings so that it can be adjusted." Nadine put Crista's finger first on the f-stop that controlled aperture and then on the shutter speed that controlled how quickly the shutter opened and closed when the picture was finally shot.

"You must have been good with a camera," Crista said to Nadine as she adjusted and focused on the kids lying in the playpen on the front lawn of the cabin. It wasn't much of a lawn, with grass only here and there in tufts, but that's what Nadine called it.

"Oh, I only did family stuff," she said, "though one photo I took appeared in the paper. I have it inside in a scrapbook. But unfortunately I left the camera at home with my parents. It was a Minolta and cost me a fortune when I finally plunked down my money to buy it at a local shop."

"Well, I want to know everything you know," Crista said as she snapped the photo. There was no film in the camera yet. She didn't want to waste it.

"Be prepared to spend a lot of money on film and developing. In every strip of twenty-four or thirty-six pictures, you might get one that's really good. And only one in a hundred could come close to being worth hanging up. Probably only one in five hundred or a thousand would be worth publishing in a book like that one your dad gave you."

"You're kidding!"

"Of course not," Nadine said, raising her blonde eyebrows and shaking her head. "It's tough to get a good photo of anything. You're used to Mom and Dad snapping pics of the family. But real photographers have to spend a lot of time learning their craft. It's a craft, just like making pottery or carpentry or whatever."

Crista crimped her lips with astonishment. "I never thought of it that way. I'd better start doing more babysitting and selling more paintings if I'm going to make it as a photographer. All that film will be expensive."

"Yeah," Nadine replied, "and then you've got all the competition."

Crista sighed. "I'm not going to set the world on fire here. Just take a few photos, that's all. Maybe use them for my painting."

"Whatever you do," Nadine said, "I'm sure it'll be exceptional."

"You're just prejudiced."

"Right."

Crista walked around the yard snapping pretend photos of various things—a little flower budding up out of a rotten log, some moss, a mushroom here and there, the way new leaves on a tree etched against the sky. It was fun and exhilarating. Nadine posed with the children by the clothesline, in front of the cabin door, on the bench. She threw back her hair professionally and moved about like a model as Crista jumped and leaped around getting angles and light the way she wanted it. After nearly an hour of this, she said, "I think I'm ready to do some real shooting."

"It's your money," Nadine replied. "How many rolls do you have?"

"Two. Thirty-six prints each."

"That's good. You'll use them up quickly."

They both stepped inside the house with the babies and sat down at the heavy polished oaken table. Big brown knots broke up the flat tan of the oak. Nadine set the little ones on a blue blanket spread out on the kitchen floor. Breaking out two Cokes, Nadine snapped the caps off with a can opener. She bought them cheap at a local factory, and the bottles were returnable. She set one down in front of Crista.

Opening the camera's back casing, Crista loaded in the Kodak film she was using. "Did you ever think of being a real photographer?" Crista asked Nadine as the older woman sipped her Coke and stuck a bare toe into Fairlight's side as she lay on the blanket. The little girl giggled and Crista smiled affectionately at the two children. Crista wanted to steer away from talking about the bear. She didn't want Nadine to be any more frightened than she already was. Anyway, there had been no more visitations that Nadine knew of.

"Oh, all I ever wanted to do was be married to Johnny and have kids," Nadine said.

"Really?" Crista was kind of surprised. "I would think you could be real ambitious when you want to."

"I can. About my kids. My home. My husband."

"Oh." Crista paused for a moment. "I just thought you may have wanted to do something different."

Nadine gazed at Crista thoughtfully. "I think you only have one life to live in this world, and you have to decide pretty early what you want out of it. Make a mistake at the beginning and it could really cost you years down the road. You know, you hear about women today who want to have children, but they're in their late thirties or even their forties and they're wondering if they missed something. I think it's good to get it figured out early. But sometimes I wonder if what most people want is what they *really* long for, or whether they're just listening to all the magazine and TV people who seem to think a big splashy career is all anybody could ever want."

"But didn't you ever want a career, Nadine?"

"I have a career—right here."

"But I mean..."

"I know what you mean and that's just the point. Being a wife and mother is as much a career as directing a movie or being an attorney or running a machine in the factory."

"I know, but..."

"No, you don't know." Nadine leaned closer, looking into Crista's eyes. "You're only twelve years old. And you want to be an artist and a photographer, and all that. That's okay. But there comes a time for each of us when we have to reevaluate, to take a real look at what we're doing with this life God has given us. I don't think God will be real concerned about whether we won the Pulitzer prize or the third race at Bristol or whether we got in *Vogue* magazine or *Seventeen*. What God is concerned about is what you did with what you were given and where you were placed. If He's really there, and I believe He is and that He gave me everything I am and have, then He wants me to use it right, for Him, for His glory. So..."

"I didn't know you believed that way, Nadine," Crista interrupted.

"Oh, yeah, I'm a Christian from way back."

Her eyes suddenly tearing, Crista said, "My mom was a Christian—or should I say is a Christian, but only in heaven. And so is my dad."

"What about you?"

"I was baptized last year when I decided to believe, too. But sometimes I wonder if it really took."

"What do you mean?" Nadine was studying Crista's eyes and face.

"Well, nothing big really happened. I just prayed that Jesus would take hold of my life and that was about it. I confessed some sins, too, the ones I knew about. And I thought about it a long time before I did it. But it seems sometimes like I wonder if He's really there or not."

"You know how you know?"

Crista's eyes came up to Nadine's. "How?"

"When you read the Bible, do you feel like it gives you hope and encouragement? If it does that, then you've got the real thing. Sometimes it convicts you right down to your toes, and that's another side. And sometimes it says something that sticks with you. That's the test."

"Yeah, that happens to me. Not all the time."

"It doesn't have to happen all the time. Just when you need it. Another thing is when you pray, do you really feel you're talking to someone? Is there a sense that it's not a game, or not a thing you're just doing, but that God is really listening?"

"Yeah, most of the time."

"Well, then that's it," Nadine said. "Being a Christian is having a relationship. Kind of like with Johnny. Sometimes it's up. Sometimes it's down. Sometimes he's talking a lot, or I'm talking a lot, and sometimes we're silent, just enjoying being together. And then sometimes we're mad at each other, too. Then we give each other the silent treatment. I pretend he's not there, that sort of thing. But when you're in a relationship, you keep coming back, making up, changing, listening, and talking. If you're doing that, then you have a real relationship."

Crista's throat felt tight for a moment. She'd talked about these things before—to her dad and in church— but not with Nadine. Then she stood and walked over and hugged Nadine suddenly. "I really love you, Nay."

"I love you, too."

"Thanks for telling me that. It really helped."

"Good."

They parted and suddenly turned and looked at the kids. Both of them were staring up at the twosome as if enchanted.

"Well, what do you know!" Nadine said. "A little talk, a little hug, and suddenly they're interested."

Crista laughed.

"All right, now what were we talking about?" Nadine said.

"Life, I think," Crista answered.

"Right. Now let me get out lecture number sixteen hundred and thirty-six and we'll continue."

They both laughed, then walked to the door and stared outside. Crista wondered briefly if the bear sat out there somewhere watching them. She shivered a little at the thought. Then she looked at Johnny Junior He looked fine, but Nadine had told her earlier that once he was past fifteen pounds the doctors would operate.

Her throat was tight again. She felt Nadine's eyes on her. After a silence, Nadine asked, "Are you okay, Crista? You look like you've seen a ghost."

Crista shook her head. "Just thinking about Johnny Junior and his hernia."

"Yeah, I think about it all the time."

Crista looked into Nadine's eyes. "He couldn't die, could he?"

"I don't know." Nadine choked suddenly and Crista leaned over and took her hand.

"Are you okay?"

Nadine shook her head. "I'm scared. Really scared."

Crista set her lips. "Well, God is watching out for you. Something will happen. You'll get the money."

Nadine nodded. "Yeah, I hope."

·8·

Picture of a Grizzly

Later that afternoon, Crista invited Lindy over to her house for a photo session. She made Rontu and Tigger sit in front of the big tool and storage box down by the lake behind her cabin. Crista stepped back with Lindy. "Now smile, you guys!"

She pressed the button and the shutter snapped.

"Perfect!" Lindy cried. "Now me!"

"I've already taken twelve of you!" Crista said.

"Yeah, but you need more. Remember what Nadine told you—only one in a hundred is really super. And I shouldn't be anything less than super!"

Rolling her eyes, Crista pushed Lindy toward the two dogs. "All right, make a pose. Something cute."

Lindy stooped down and grabbed both dogs' heads. Rontu was a tall, milk-white great dane with crystal-blue eyes. Tigger was a little shelty, about one-third the height of Rontu, and he had brown fur with white mixed in. He only had one eye. The missing eye left an ugly gouge in his face, but Crista had managed to clean him up since his "dump dog" days and he looked presentable, even a bit handsome. All he needed was a black patch and he'd make a perfect pirate or desperado.

Lindy pressed both canine faces against her cheek and said, "Lick, boys."

Crista caught both of them with long slurpy tongues hanging out against Lindy's cheeks. Lindy laughed, then stood and wiped herself off. "How was that?"

"Fine," Crista said, putting down her camera.

"Oh, not yet!" Lindy answered. She struck a model pose, her head thrown back, her neck glistening in the sunlight. "Get that."

Crista shot.

Moving quickly to another position, set on her toes about to dive, Lindy said, "And that!"

Crista shot.

Again, Lindy swerved around, throwing out her leg.

"Okay, okay, film costs money, Lindy, and I only have one roll left after I finish this one. I really wish I could get a picture of the bear."

"Yeah, that would be great."

They traipsed up through the woods by the lake. No one was allowed to walk in the woods across the road until the bear was captured. Crista, Lindy, and Jeff made the most of it by sticking to the fringe of the woods around the lake behind the houses. It was fairly certain the bear would not show up down there, even though the search team had been all over Moonlight Mountain the day before. It looked like Vic the grizzly had discovered how to play hide-and-seek fairly well. No one had seen him since he'd escaped three days before—except that one moment at Nadine's. But of course no one was sure it had been a bear or anything else, let alone the escaped grizzly.

Crista zeroed in on different kinds of light sifting through the trees, the way a branch or some leaves etched the sky, and different kinds of bark. They stopped at one of the docks hauled up on the beach for the winter and sat down on top of it. The two dogs sniffed and trotted around the area, looking for all the world like this was another picnic. Which more or less was precisely what it was, minus food.

"I wonder how they would capture a bear like that," Lindy said, hugging her knees and rocking as the twosome sat on the dock. Crista continued looking through the camera viewfinder and roving the beach for something to shoot.

"Probably with a net or something."

"Yeah, but maybe he'll like being in the woods on his own. And maybe he won't want to go back."

Crista turned to her and nodded. "Yeah, that's true. I guess if he didn't like the woods life, he would have given himself up by now."

Lindy laughed. "Given himself up? Like in the movies, huh?"

"Yeah." Crista turned sideways and zoomed in on Lindy's face. "You have a good face," she said.

"Yeah, I know."

"Oh, the modest one."

Lindy grinned. "No, my dad says I'm exceptionally cute."

"Way to help you become humble!"

Smiling, Lindy gave her a little punch in the shoulder. "I'm humble."

"Oh, yeah! And I'm Miss America."

Lindy gazed at Crista, almost startled. "I bet you could be."

"Oh, come on."

"No, Crista. I'm cute. But you're beautiful."

"Get off it."

"No, really. You have great eyes."

Crista looked away. "Let's talk about something else."

"Okay." Lindy shimmied off the dock and dropped to the ground. Behind them, there was a sudden chittering and she turned her gaze to the storage box. "Hey, look. Two squirrels, fighting."

"That might be interesting."

Crista jumped off the dock and swung around, catching the two squirrels in a head-to-head, arm-in-arm pose. It looked like they were kissing. As she pressed the shutter button, the larger squirrel, a fat gray one, shoved the other one off the box. It rolled, came up on its feet, and leaped.

"Boy, he's a frisky one," Crista said as she took another shot.

"Yeah," Lindy said. Suddenly, she whipped around. "I know!"

Stopping her mad rush to get as many shots of the squirrels as possible, Crista let down the camera. "What?"

"I know where we can get a picture of a bear."

"Where?"

"Mr. Belfield."

"Who's he?"

"He lives on our road between us and the Wilkinses."

"So what can he do?"

Lindy clapped her hands. "Yeah! He has all kinds of animals in his living room. Mounted. A moose. And some deer, like Johnny and Nadine have. A bobcat, too. Two white mountain goats. Oh, and a pig."

"A pig?"

"Not a pig, though. You know. With the curly teeth."

Crista nodded. "A wild boar!"

"Yeah!" Lindy's eyes were wide.

"So what about the bear?"

"I bet he has one."

Crista shook her head. "You mean you don't know if he has one?"

"I never saw it. But I was only in there once. I bet he has a bear. Daddy says he's a big hunter—or he used to be years ago when you could hunt animals and stuff. I bet he even has a grizzly."

"Well, then, let's go!"

"All right!"

·9·

Mr. Belfield

"It's kind of a scary-looking house," Crista said as they both stood on Rock Road, having walked past the Wilkinses' farm, and peered down the long driveway to Mr. Belfield's. "Does he live alone?"

"I guess," Lindy said. She didn't look as eager now as she had before.

They had already called Lindy's mother at the restaurant to see if it would be all right for them to drop by Mr. Belfield's. Since he was a friend of the Helstroms, Mrs. Helstrom said it was fine, as long as they returned home by five-thirty.

The house stood tall and shadowy, set back in the trees, with several large boulders in the front yard. It looked like it had sprouted right up out of the ground. A genuine log cabin, it had mud-like cement caulking the spaces between the logs. It was two stories high, and an American flag waved from the very top. There, high above them, towered a parapet that looked like the corner of some fort where soldiers with muskets fought off Indians in the days before the Revolutionary War.

"Did he build it?" Crista asked. She slung the camera over her shoulder, ready for action. There were only about ten photos left, but she wanted to see some

67

of the trophies, even though she didn't like animals' heads hanging from a wall like that.

"I think so. A really long time ago. Like before the earth completely formed," Lindy said.

Crista laughed. "Where do you get these jokes?"

Lindy said, "It's my special talent." She made a goofy face, then turned around. "Guess we should just go up and knock."

"Are you sure you want to do this?"

"Yeah, I guess. What can he do? Shoot us and hang us on the wall with the other animals?"

Again, Crista laughed. "He just might!"

"Yeah, that's what I like about going here. It scares the heebie-jeebies out of me, like Jeff says."

"Well, I'm glad you can admit that, because I'm feeling about the same way."

After a pause, waiting for the other to make the move, Crista finally said, "Okay, come on. But you'll have to introduce me."

Mr. Belfield was burly and he wore a leather jerkin. His eyes twinkled like Santa Claus's, and he wore a goatee like Colonel Sanders of Kentucky Fried Chicken fame. In fact, he actually looked a little like the Colonel, except his hair was gray, not white, and he wasn't fat at all.

"Well, Lindy, I haven't seen you in weeks," he said, greeting them both with a smile.

Lindy stood there, tongue-tied for once, then she stammered, "Th-this is my tutor, Crista Mayfield. She wants to take pictures of your animals. And we were hoping you had at least one bear, hopefully a grizzly."

Crista smiled and Mr. Belfield laughed like his belly was a bowlful of jelly, and he invited them in. "You're sure you won't be scared now?"

"Nah, my mom knows where we are, so if you shoot us and hang us up with the animals she'll come and take us back."

He laughed again, a deep, thick-chested laugh that made Crista think of a bowlful of moose meat, not jelly. Crista smiled as she stepped through. The house smelled of pipe smoke, garlic, and tomatoes. Crista thought he must have been smoking his pipe while tending a pot of fresh spaghetti sauce. The house was laid out like typical cabins with an immediate main room doubling as living room and dining room, a large picture window in the back, and a stone fireplace. Over the fireplace hung a monster moose head. And the moose's lips sported a giant cigar. It made Crista cover her mouth and stifle a laugh.

Lindy said, "Mr. Belfield believes in letting them die before they smoke."

Mr. Belfield led them inside. "So you want to see a bear, huh?"

"Yup," Lindy answered, nodding her head. "Whatever you got."

He led them up a flight of stairs and into one of the back bedrooms. "I like to keep him right over my head—this one anyway. I have two others in the other bedrooms, but since you're interested in a grizzly I'll show you Bubbles first."

"Bubbles!" Lindy and Crista exclaimed together.

"Yeah." Mr. Belfield picked a pipe up off the dresser and lit it. The girls gazed up at the big bear head. "I like to give all my friends pet names. Then we can have a real relationship, the kind we never had in real life." He smiled and Crista realized it was a joke. But Lindy just stood there with her mouth open.

"I call him Bubbles because when I found him the first time he stood in the river trying to catch a trout and blowing bubbles left and right. He was a real bubble blower. Could have been a clown in the circus." Mr. Belfield looked up at the bear affectionately.

The trophy was a giant brown and grizzled head with the same kind of silverish color the circus bears had. His mouth opened wide in a majestic snarl with the lips pulled back, and large incisors and fangs protruded. A thick red tongue bunched back into the mouth as if the bear was growling just before pouncing. Black lips shadowed the stark white teeth. It was a scary sight.

Both girls stared up at the bear. Crista couldn't imagine meeting that brute in a dream let alone real life. Even a gun wouldn't seem like much protection in that situation. She shivered unconsciously. The idea of ever meeting Vic in the woods and saving him from the hunters fled.

"Why do you have him just above your bed?" Crista asked, her voice nearly trembling.

The old man looked up at the bear with twinkly eyes. "Oh, he brings back so many fond memories."

"Fond memories?" Crista said with a gulp. She glanced at Lindy who had moved back and stared up at the bear as if he stood at the top of a ten-story building. All Crista could think of was walking through the woods scared to death with a gun in your hands and then having this beast charge while you tried to remember how to aim the gun! If you survived the fight, and didn't lose your cookies at the same time, she guessed you would have a story to tell.

"Sure. We hunters always have great memories of the time we got this one or that one or the other one.

That's why you have a trophy. It's not just to show him off—like you're someone really tough because you shot a poor little bear—but there's a special sort of relationship there that is undefinable."

Both Crista and Lindy stared at Mr. Belfield as if he was from outer space.

"It's a hunting thing," he finally said. "So have you seen enough?"

"Can I take a picture?" Crista asked uneasily.

"Sure. You want him and me together? Should I take him down so you can get real close? What's your pleasure?"

"Just like he is now is okay."

"All right."

Everyone stood back as Crista snapped a couple pictures using her flash, and then stood on one of the chairs in the room so she could get a close-up. "He really looks fierce," she said as she jumped down.

"That he was, that he was."

There was an uneasy silence. Then Mr. Belfield said, "You want to know how I got him?"

Crista swallowed and she glanced at Lindy. The little girl stood big-eyed and obviously curious.

"Definitely," Lindy cried.

Crista was a bit more evasive. "Is it scary?"

"You bet!" answered the old man.

"Okay," Crista finally said.

"All right, you two sit over there on the bench and I'll sit on the bed." The bear hung over the middle of the bed, high on the wall only a foot from the ceiling. Other than that, the room held just a dresser and a rifle on bent deer hooves hanging over the dresser mirror. It appeared to be a twenty-two. Johnny Semms had one that looked a little like it.

"Now first we have to get something settled," Mr. Belfield said. "Do you want the souped-up version or the plain bread-and-gravy version?"

"Oh, the souped-up one," Lindy said right away.

"Then you'll have to put up with a little of my storytelling," Mr. Belfield said. He sat down, extended his legs, and squinted at the two girls, looking tough as nails and ready to kill to boot. The look made Crista's spine prickle with excitement. What kind of story was this going to be?

·10·

Mr. Belfield's Story

"I was coming through the woods. I'd seen him one time before in the creek, hunting trout. But I didn't have the big gun with me, and I didn't want to take a chance of wounding him. So I had come back to see if I could find his lair.

"He was big. Had to be a good nine hundred to a thousand pounds. Probably six or seven years old. A young one. Not many left in those days. They were hunted down and destroyed and I felt—well, I didn't feel real good about going after him."

He motioned to the bear and looked up a moment, then nodded.

"Yeah, he was the last of a breed." Mr. Belfield's eyes almost teared a moment, then he looked back at the kids. "Anyway, on with the story.

"I come up through the trees and saw an area strewn with rocks. I'd tracked him several different times, but had never seen him except that one time. And I'd never seen this area of rocks before. It was way up in Montana near the Canadian border—I came out there for a special trip with some friends. I'd been out most of the day and hadn't seen anything, not even a deer, though I wasn't after deer."

The old man had a far-off look in his eyes. Crista could tell it was an emotional story for him.

"I walked up through the rocks, going real slow, taking a few steps and listening, a few more steps and listening. My heart was pounding. I knew I was close to something, but not sure what. I was afraid he'd not be there and it'd be a wild goose chase. And then I was afraid he *would* be there and he'd just pop up and bite my face off before I had a chance to even sneeze."

Both girls laughed uneasily. It was already a good story. Crista thought she might invite Mr. Belfield to come down to the school and tell the same story to the class. He seemed a little lonely. His cheeks flamed a rose red as he talked, and he seemed to be far away, back in that place, reliving it as he told it.

"I wound around through the rocks. Then I saw it— a cave. I knew in my gut this was it. He was in there, or had been there anyway. I could wait till he came out and then pick him off. But he might not come out till dark, and I didn't want to be that far from home base when night fell. So I edged closer. I made some bear calls I learned years ago."

He stopped and pursed his lips, then cupped his hands around his mouth and made a fierce, growly, howling sound. It chilled Crista right down to her toe tips.

"I waited. Nothing happened. I checked my rifle over and over. Big gun with bear load. Really kicks when you fire that baby. More than two or three shots and I'd call it a day. My shoulder would hurt for a week.

"I also had a nine millimeter Beretta pistol in a holster on my hip, and a bowie knife on my belt behind me. I touched both, as if for luck, and then waited some more. I knew I had to go inside, see if he was there anyway. It was a big cave with a wide mouth, and I could already see in a few feet. But if he was sleeping, I didn't hear any snoring noises or anything like that. So I stood there, trying to control my breathing. I had my gun up at my shoulder and advanced. Very slowly. Step. Stop. Listen. Wait. Sight in. Then another step."

"Were you scared?" Lindy asked suddenly.

"My heart was thumping so loud I thought they must be able to hear it in Manitoba."

"Manitoba?" Lindy said, glancing at Crista.

"One of the provinces in Canada," Mr. Belfield said and paused to draw deeply on his pipe.

His eyes twinkled and he smiled. "Yeah, I was real scared."

Both girls waited as he adjusted his pipe. "I didn't know whether I should advance any further. I stood right in the mouth of the cave. And then I heard it. A rumble. A low growl. He was there. But he wasn't in the cave!"

Crista's eyes grew big and her heart pounded into her mouth as she listened. Where was that bear?

"He was behind me! Standing up. I could feel his breath on my neck. I knew with one swipe, I'd be done for. So I just stood there."

"Just stood there with him behind you!" Lindy cried.

"Yup. What else could I do? He had me. He'd snuck up and I was so concentrated on finding him that I didn't hear a thing. So you know what I did?"

"What?" both girls said.

"I said to him, 'What you gonna do, big boy?'"

"What did he do then?"

"He growled again. Maybe he was as scared as I was. But I knew I had to make a move. I was too close for the rifle. So I slowly moved my hand back to my pistol. And that was when he let it rip!"

Both girls sat up straight. Mr. Belfield's face was dark with the menace of the bear.

"That paw felt like a Joe Louis right hook. I went up through the air and my rifle clattered right to the ground, useless. The bear stood up over me, his paws out, as if inviting me to put up my dukes. I fumbled for my gun. This was no longer hunting. This was a duel to the death. I rolled over and the bear slapped me down with his paw, almost raking my face."

He stood now and walked to the headboard of the bed. He gestured with his hands wildly.

"I unsnapped the strap that held my gun in its holster. A second later I had it out. But the bear was faster. With a great sweep of his left paw, he batted my hand. The claws ripped into my wrist. The gun slapped right out of it, clunking to the dirt, ten feet away."

"You were dead meat!" Lindy exclaimed.

"Exactly. The only weapon I had left was my knife. And I was lying on it. The bear snarled above me, menacing, determined to kill me and probably eat me for dinner. But I moved as quickly as I could. I twisted around, grabbed the handle of the knife and drew it out. The bear advanced. Suddenly, he fell on my shoulders, pinning me to the ground. His hot breath gusted into my face. He snarled, reared back, and howled. The kill roar—what I imagine bears always do before ripping out the throat of a victim. I had no strength left. He had me. But I couldn't give up.

"The bear looked at me with those two glowing brown eyes, then roared again. It was over, unless . . ."

Crista couldn't move or think. She simply gaped. Mr. Belfield fell on the bed and acted like he was pinned under the bear. He shook his head with fright.

"Unless?" both girls cried, the suspense killing them.

"Unless, I could drive that knife right into his heart."

He paused, breathing slower, closing his eyes. "I pulled my arm up against the weight. The bear dove. Flattened me. Going for my throat. A split second later, I would have been dead. But I drove that knife deep into his chest."

He thrust out as if jabbing the knife into the bear's chest.

"Blood gushed all over me. The bear pulled back, stood up. The knife stuck out of his chest like a lance. He screamed. And then he toppled over, one paw over my extended leg. I jumped up, ran for my pistol and turned around with it in my hand, ready to fire. I waited. The bear didn't move. It was over. He was dead!"

Mr. Belfield sat down and sighed. "It was the fight of my life, kids!"

"Wow!" Lindy said, looking up at the bear. "And he almost put your head up in his cave and made you his trophy."

"That's right." Mr. Belfield's eyes twinkled and he smiled. Crista gazed at him and she sensed something else was afoot, though. She waited.

Lindy said, "That's the bravest story I ever heard!"

Mr. Belfield shook his head. "Well, actually . . ." He looked away, drew on his pipe, then leaned forward. "Can I tell you a secret?"

Both girls pulled in closer. The confidentiality made Crista feel important.

"That's not what really happened."

"It isn't?" Lindy whispered.

"It was like this!" Suddenly he squeezed both girls at the tickle point in the ribs, and they fell back, laughing.

Mr. Belfield sat back on the bed. His face crinkled and he said, with a little grin, "I can't tell a lie, kids. That really is a partly made-up story, right out of Grizzly Adams."

"Grizzly Adams?" Lindy said questioningly. Crista instantly remembered what Mr. Turner had said about the great American hunter and entertainer.

"Grizzly Adams was a great old hunter and performer of the nineteenth century. He caught bears and other animals for circuses and zoos around the world, then put together his own show, called The California Menagerie. Finally ended up with P.T. Barnum, the great circus man. To advertise the show, he used to get his three grizzlies on a wagon and drive around. Then he'd sit on the shoulders of one of them and have the two others on either side of him on leashes—and all that with nothing on them, not even muzzles. He was one brave man."

Crista suddenly said, "That's exactly what Mr. Turner said he does."

"Who's Mr. Turner?" the old man asked.

"The trainer of the bears. Don't you know about the circus and the bear loose in the woods?"

"The one mentioned in the papers?"

"Yes."

"Oh, yes, I read about it," Mr. Belfield said. "I was even thinking about offering my services. But I figured they had enough gunslingers running around."

Crista continued when the old man paused, "Mr. Turner said he sits on Vic's shoulders in his show."

Mr. Belfield rubbed his chin. "Dangerous thing to do with a live bear. The man must have real guts."

"I think he does," Crista said.

Mr. Belfield suddenly looked very serious. "The point is, killing wild animals isn't a happy business, kids. Today, fortunately, there are restrictions. And people like your Mr. Turner are doing something far better through their shows. But when I used to hunt, it was a way for a man to prove how tough he was, or so we thought. No, I shot Bubbles at thirty yards. Never got close enough to smell him—until after he was dead. It wasn't a great act of bravery like I like to think."

Crista was surprised, but Mr. Belfield said, "You know, I'm a little ashamed of how I shot Bubbles now. If it had been in self-defense, maybe it would have justified the killing. I've changed, though. I have all these trophies in the house, but now they're a badge of shame. I never should have killed those animals just to mount their heads and make myself look brave. You should never kill for those reasons, even a wild beast like that one."

He smiled at the two girls, then touched their heads. "So I hope you're not too disappointed. But that's how I tell the story to my grandchildren, and then I tell them the truth. Every man likes to think of himself as braver than he is. But shooting a wild beast at thirty yards with a high-powered rifle isn't particularly brave in my book anymore."

"You really love animals now, huh," Crista said, feeling a special friendship toward the man.

"Yeah. Wouldn't hurt them for the world."

"What do you know about the grizzly in the woods?"

He shook his head. "Just what I heard on the news and read in the paper. Feel kinda sorry for him. Some trigger-happy guy who wants to think of himself as brave will probably end up shooting him. But I hope it's not that way."

He led them downstairs. "Would you like a cookie and some cola, kids?"

"No," Crista answered. "We need to get home. But thanks, Mr. Belfield. We liked your story. Do you think you could come to our school sometime and tell one?"

"Sure, sure. Anytime."

He stood in the doorway and waved as the girls went down the driveway. "I liked his first story better," Lindy said when they reached the road.

"Yeah, so did he. But I'm glad he told us the truth."

"Yeah, I guess."

Crista wondered, though, if the police and people trying to track the bear wouldn't be wise to ask Mr. Belfield for help.

·11·

At Nadine's

That night, Crista and Jeff planned to babysit at Nadine and Johnny's while the couple went out and celebrated their first-date anniversary. Johnny picked them both up in his truck about seven-fifteen, well after dark. It was early April, just before daylight savings time, so it still turned dark about six-thirty. It looked to be a cloudless night, and Jeff, Crista, and Johnny talked about the bear, the circus, and how Johnny had gotten a new job at a Jiffy Lube in Honesdale.

"It pays decent, too," Johnny said. "First time I've gotten decent pay since we've been here."

"Have you ever thought about going to college?" Jeff asked Johnny. The three of them sat in the cab of the truck, a bit mashed together. The truck was cobalt blue—Crista knew that from painting—and it was Johnny's third love, after Nadine and the twins.

"Nah," Johnny said to the question about college. "I'm not good at that stuff."

"But wouldn't it make it easier on you, if you had a degree?" Crista broke in. She had been thinking about the Semms' need of money for Johnny Junior's operation. She knew neither Johnny nor Nadine had much hope of bettering their lives in any way without college. At least that was what the teachers said at school, and her dad, too. She knew college wasn't the answer to everything, but from what she'd seen, Johnny had no marketable skills except basketball and hunting. Still, she didn't want to nag him, even if it was the first time they'd mentioned it.

"It probably would," Johnny said. "But college costs money and that's one thing we haven't got any of."

Crista thought again of Nadine's fondness for photography. Maybe that was something. Maybe she could get Nadine to try it again, too. They could work together on a project.

Johnny turned down the road past the dump, and they bumped along saying little. Crista let her gaze rest on the woods. She wondered where the bear was and if he'd been captured that afternoon. "Hear anything about the bear?" she said, not really expecting much of an answer.

"Another search party going up. Now they're going out at night because they think he's holed up somewhere during the day. Setting up some traps with meat and stuff. But some of them are saying he's traveled."

"How far?" Jeff asked.

"These woods stretch for miles, man," Johnny said. "It's been over three days now. He could be going to Canada. Maybe he's even got a map. Stole one from the circus."

Jeff and Crista laughed.

"But I think he's still here."

"You do?"

"Yeah. I saw some tracks yesterday."

Jeff and Crista turned their heads simultaneously. "Where?" Jeff asked.

"Up the road. I was walking with my gun, just looking around, and I saw some unmistakable bear tracks. Going right across the road not far from the dump. Not going fast, either. So I think he's still here. Who else could have made those tracks?"

"Are you sure they were fresh?"

"There were some tire tracks over them, but just one set. Made between last night and this morning, I think."

"You don't think he'd come around while we're at the cabin, do you?" Crista asked, a little shake in her voice.

"Don't know. But you gotta couple guns in the house. Jeff knows how to use them—right, Jeff?"

Jeff nodded. "You'll leave some shells, too, right?"

"Yeah, I'll show you. But I don't think he'll be around. And I don't want you playing around with it, Jeff."

"Right."

"Only in a real emergency."

"Of course."

"But you don't want to shoot him anyway," Crista added, "because there's a $500 reward." She told Johnny about Cal Turner's offer. It would be wonderful if Johnny got it *and* saved the bear at the same time.

Nadine and Johnny left at seven-thirty. She was dressed, as she usually was when she went out, in a stylish two-year-old lacy creme outfit with pearl buttons down the front and high heels. Jeff had never seen Nadine look like that, and Crista simply stood back and grinned as he gaped. Johnny had on a tweed jacket with open-necked shirt and jeans. He still could not abide regular dress pants.

Before she left, Nadine said, "Johnny Junior's been throwing up everything. I think I gave him too much to eat. The doctor says I can only give him a little at a time because of the hernia. So watch him close, please.

I'm taking him in tomorrow morning to see the doc. He shouldn't get sick again, but if he does, just sit him up and pat his back."

Crista nodded. "We'll take care of him."

When they were gone, Jeff took up residence on the little couch in the living room and checked out Johnny's rifle, sighting through the scope into the yard, looking through the barrel to check for flecks of gunpowder— there were none because Johnny always cleaned his rifle shortly after using it—and rubbing it with a chamois wipe that Johnny had given him. Crista didn't like him looking out the window with the gun like that, but at least he was not aiming at anything and it wasn't loaded. And if the bear did come around, at least she could trust that if it came to a battle, Jeff could shoot the gun at it. Johnny had suggested simply firing it into the air.

The twins were asleep in the bedroom. No sound but a gentle breathing fluttered from them. Only the wind-up clock on the mantel made any noise. Crista thumbed through her photography book and prac- ticed with her camera, pretending to do close-up photos of everything from the dirty dishes in the sink to the sleeping twosome in Johnny and Nadine's bedroom.

The Semms had no television, so Crista finally turned their little Panasonic boom box on and plugged in a tape Nadine had of eighties hits. The first tune was one Nadine liked by Elton John called "Candle in the Wind," and Crista sank back in the deep cushioned armchair Johnny had rescued from the dump and listened. She was soon singing the songs, not noticing that Jeff had fallen asleep on the couch clutching the rifle to his chest like it was a kiddie blanket he had not yet outgrown.

The music filled her mind as she lay back in the chair, curled up, and closed her eyes. A dreamy feeling of floating calmed her. It felt like lying on a rubber raft in the water with the sun on your face and the rolls of water gently shushing you up and down till you fell asleep.

Crista was first aware of pinging, tinkly sounds as if at the end of a long tunnel. She awoke with a start.

"Jeff? Jeff!"

Instantly, Jeff rolled off the couch with the rifle still clutched in his arms. "What?"

"There's something making noise at the back of the cabin. Trash cans or something."

"What?" Jeff pulled himself together, set down the gun on the woven rag carpet, and stood up. He rubbed his eyes, then listened. Crista rose and realized the tape had run out. All was silent.

They both walked stealthily through the living room to the back bedroom where the twins were. Reaching the window, they peered out into the darkness and listened. Johnny still had not set the screens in. The enclosed glass window muffled whatever noises were out there.

"Don't open this window," Crista said. "If it's something out there, we should go up in the loft and open that window. It can't get to that one as easily."

"Okay," Jeff said, turning around.

"Lock the front door," Crista said.

"I'm getting the gun," Jeff replied.

"Don't be stupid. We don't know if it's anything."

There was a sudden abrupt sound of a trash can spilling over.

"It's not anything, huh?" Jeff said.

"Wait. It could be some dump dogs. Let's go up to the loft, open the window, and look out. We don't need to go starting a fight when there isn't one."

"Okay, but I'm getting ready."

They walked silently and swiftly out of the bedroom. Being careful to leave the door open, they rushed up the loft stairs. The loft was a large open room just under the roof. Many of the local cabins had lofts. They were great for sleeping a group of people— ten or more at a shot. And it was a simple way to keep the house cool in summer.

When they reached the top, without turning on the light, Crista hurried to the back and unlatched the lock, then pulled up the lower half of the window. The trash cans boomed and clanked as if they were being thrown around at will. A loud snuffling noise filled the air. Trembling, Crista and Jeff stuck their heads out. Directly below them in the moonlight was a huge furry animal, unmistakably a bear.

The grizzly. His silver fur shone in the moonlight. He nosed around in the cans, throwing things left and right as he sniffed for food. He didn't look very fierce under the stars, even kind of cuddly—like one of those stuffed bears you could buy in the toy store.

"He's hungry," Crista said, pulling inside. "Maybe we should give him something."

"Maybe we should get the sheriff and get him captured," Jeff whispered. They both kept their voices down, but obviously the bear heard. A rumbly growl broke the quiet.

Freezing, Crista slowly leaned back out the window. Greeting her was the bear's face, less than five feet below. He was standing up, stretched out, his paws extended. His red tongue lolled out and he threw his head back.

"Awroooooooooooow!"

Crista fell back and Jeff caught her.

"He's right up the side of the building," she cried.

"I'm getting the gun," Jeff said, letting her down onto the floor.

"No!" Crista yelled, sitting down. "No guns."

Jeff gave her a strained look, then shook his head.

Crista crept back to the window and slowly drew herself up. Jeff went downstairs to get the twins.

As she came back up to the view, she looked out, then down. The bear wasn't there.

"He's gone!" Crista shouted and ran to the stairs, leaning out over the banister. "He's not there!"

Jeff had the twins on the couch. He picked up the gun.

"Put down the gun, Jeff! He's gone."

"I'm going outside to check it out."

Crista rushed down the stairs. "Don't start trouble where there is no trouble," she said angrily as Jeff walked to the door. "You heard what Mr. Turner said."

"I'm not starting trouble. The bear could still be dangerous!"

"He is not. You saw him. He's just hungry."

Immediately, there was a roar outside, this time in the front yard.

"Awrrooooooooooow!"

Both kids froze. One of the twins awoke and started crying. Crista rolled Johnny Junior over on the couch and the child was instantly asleep again, his thumb jammed between his lips.

Jeff stood at the window, squinting out into the night. Beyond the light of the cabin it was dark, but in the moonlight and starlight, things could be seen to the edge of the trees—Johnny's woodpile in the front yard, a small shed on the edge of the woods, and an old green wheelbarrow sagging onto its side.

Then suddenly, Jeff was laughing. "Come here, Crista. You have to see this!"

Crista walked over to the window. Jeff pointed, then walked to the front door and stepped out. "I have to get a better view of this."

Jeff stood on the porch and Crista came up behind him.

The moonlight shone down in steep trunks of quicksilver. The whole cleared area in front of the house looked lit up. And in the center stood the grizzly. He reached up into the sky while standing on his hind legs, his front paws extended over his head as if about to bow down in worship. The bear began pirouetting around in a circle.

"He's dancing," Crista whispered.

"Yeah," Jeff said. "In the moonlight."

The bear roared again as if charmed by the sight of the moon. A moment later, he plopped down on the ground and rolled over. Three times. Then he stood and hopped about on his feet. Next he somersaulted. Then rolled. Then spun.

It was incredible. Crista and Jeff had never seen anything like it.

Just as suddenly, the bear stopped, fell back onto all fours, and lifted up his right paw. He moved the paw up and down and nodded his head.

"He's waving!" Crista cried.

"Let's wave back!"

They both did.

The bear stood again, roared, then turned and ran into the trees.

"That was fantastic!" Jeff exclaimed. "I mean, he put on a little show for us."

"I know," Crista said. "It's like he knew we were the audience. Mr. Turner was right. He is almost human."

They both stared off into the woods, then went back inside, carefully locking the door. They couldn't talk about anything else, and when Johnny and Nadine came back, they poured out the whole story.

"Well, I'll be," Johnny said. "He couldn't be too out for blood then, doing that kind of thing."

"I know," Crista agreed. "And all those men are out there with their guns right now, just itching to shoot him. And poor Mr. Turner."

"We have to do something," Jeff said.

"We'll start by telling Steve what we saw," Crista decided. "First thing tomorrow morning."

·12·
The News

They called Steve Leonard early on Saturday morning. This time, he took down the whole story on tape while sitting in the Mayfields' living room. Crista's father listened raptly, saying little. Jeff spoke animatedly and exaggerated only a little about his prowess with the gun and then about how fierce the bear looked.

"He was not fierce," Crista protested. "He danced. How fierce can you be if you like dancing in the moonlight? And Mr. Turner is such a sweetie pie."

"How did he dance?" Steve asked. "Are you sure he was dancing?"

"What else could it be?" Crista replied.

"Maybe he was high on garbage," the reporter answered.

"Come on," Jeff broke in. "He's a circus bear."

"Something's wrong here," Steve said. "I did some investigating on my own yesterday and discovered that no doctor or hospital in the area has treated a bear-mauling victim within the past week. This guy Landesman or Jon Larby or whoever he is—we have to find out where he went. I think he's trying to set something up now. Since the story was in the paper, lots of people

90

are clamoring for the bear's immediate capture or destruction, whichever comes first."

"Why would that man do this?" Crista exclaimed.

Jeff leaned back in the chair and scratched his chin. "It's almost like a conspiracy or something. Do you think he was faking it? Maybe he's out to get Mr. Turner for some reason."

"It's possible this Jon Larby character is just trying to get the search moving more aggressively," Steve said. "Apparently, they haven't been real serious about it until this morning."

"But they're going to kill the bear now!" Crista almost shouted.

"That's the problem," Steve said. "Why would one of the members of the circus want them to kill the bear. Unless . . ."

"Unless?" Crista and Jeff exclaimed together.

Steve stood. "We've got to get moving. Let's get over to where all the circus people are staying, by the Richie Motel up on 590. They've got their trailers set up and some of them are staying in the motel. I think we need to find out more facts before we jump to conclusions."

"What conclusions?" Crista said, jumping out of her chair and grabbing her coat and camera. Jeff followed. "Do you think this Larby person is trying to do the bears in?"

"Why not?" Steve asked. "Maybe he's jealous. Maybe he doesn't like them and Mr. Turner. Who knows? We've got to find out. I don't know why I let this sit, but I didn't know where to look. Now I think I do."

"You three, be careful!" Crista's dad called from the doorway as Steve, Jeff, and Crista hurried out of the cabin and clambered into Steve's rusted-out Toyota Celica. "And keep me posted!"

Mashing the accelerator, Steve veered around in a semicircle and headed back out to the main road. No one said anything as they drove on 590 up to the motel. On the way, they passed the cars, police vans, and trucks still parked along the road. Only a couple of men lounged about, barely noticing them as they sliced by, Steve's little Toyota chugging like the Little Engine That Could.

"It looks like they're really going after him," Crista said, half in despair, half in hope that nothing had yet happened. If this were a setup, they had to expose it before the men found the bear, made him fight back in fear, and then ended up killing him.

"Yeah," Steve said. "But this shouldn't take long."

Five more minutes down the road they found the Richie Motel. It was stuck back from the road, nothing particularly picturesque, with red and white chipped painting. A group of little cabins and a trailer park made a cheap overnight place for people too tired or poor to scout out the Holiday Inn about ten miles in the other direction. The area behind it was crowded with the circus vehicles and many RVs and trailers, all parked in the little camper park. Most of the big trucks with animals and equipment were parked further away out of sight.

Steve parked the car and got out. It was a tight fit and Crista, sitting in the back, squeezed out after Jeff bent the front seat forward.

"Let me do the talking," Steve said.

They walked around, looking for someone to interview or at least ask a few questions. No one was about. Finally, Steve walked up to one of the RVs and knocked on the door. A moment later, a woman in curlers and a robe answered. She had a drink of brown-looking liquid with ice cubes in it in her hand.

"Yeah?" she said.

"Uh, I'm a local reporter, Steve Leonard." Steve handed her a business card with his name and title on it. Crista noticed it said, "Steve Leonard, Features Reporter" on it. She smiled, thinking how good it was that he had turned out to be friendly and not the egomaniac he'd acted like in their meeting a couple days before.

"We were wondering," Steve said, glancing at the two kids behind him, "if you know a Jon Larby."

"Yeah, what of it?" The lady took a swig of her drink and moved her lips around her teeth as if she was adjusting dentures. Crista had seen her grandfather, who also wore dentures, make the same kind of motion whenever something was "out of whack," as he put it.

"What does he do here?" Steve went on, taking notes.

"Dog trainer."

"Dog trainer?"

"Yeah, dog trainer." This lady obviously wasn't volunteering anything.

"What kind of dogs?"

"Poodles."

"What, uh, color?"

Crista could see Steve didn't know where to go with this one.

"Two blacks, two whites, and I think he's got a green one, too." The lady started to shut the door. She clearly didn't want to be questioned and was just saying what she was saying to get rid of the three of them.

"Wait a minute, please?" Steve said, stepping a little closer and getting a knee up on one of the steps into the RV.

"Look, sonny. I ain't talking about nothin', all right? This is a tight little group here and we don't want no trouble. Now, goodbye." She shut the door, brushing Steve's knee out of the way as she closed it.

When the door clicked, Steve turned to the other two. "Sounds like we got a problem with secrecy around here."

They walked around among the trailers and RVs looking for signs of life. Crista heard a radio blaring in one and touched Steve's shoulder. "Over there," she said.

They walked toward the noise. The music was rock, very loud. Jeff said, "Sounds like this guy is one of us anyway."

Steve and Crista stepped up to the little trailer and knocked. The music immediately shut off and a young man opened the door. He was shirtless and had a tanned, muscular chest and arms, a darkly handsome face, and long, black hair. Crista immediately imagined him as one of the daring young men on the flying trapeze or maybe the lion tamer. He was drinking a Coke and sported several rings on his dark fingers.

"Yes?" he said, peering out into the sunlight.

Steve introduced himself again and then asked about Jon Larby.

"Yeah, he does the dog routine. I don't know him well. I'm with the acrobats." He held out his brawny hand. "Jose Traviso."

Showing interest, Steve questioned him about his work. He said he was part of a family—the Tumbling

Travisos. He and his sisters and brothers and his mom and dad made up the troupe, and they performed mostly complex tumbling routines with all kinds of power lifts, throws, spins, and rolls through the air. He described it all graphically, commenting that he was the one who got on TV to make their commercials. "They say I articulate well." He laughed. Crista liked him.

"About Larby," Steve said. "Do you know anything about him being mauled by Vic, the escaped grizzly?"

"Larby? Nah, I saw him this morning. He was with the group going after the bear. Had his big gun. He's a hunter. But he's back now, I think."

"Do you know where he's staked out at the moment?"

"Up the road a little. An RV with a bunch of poodles on the side." He leaned out of his trailer and looked out. "Yeah, just up about six or so. What's up with Larby anyway?"

"Do you know of any trouble between him and Cal Turner, the man who owns the bears?"

"'Course. They're always in trouble. All of us are. Never enough money, never enough recognition, never enough this, never enough that. It's an endless battle. But it's a life and I like it."

"Well, thanks," Steve said.

"Anytime." Jose closed the door and Steve led them away from the trailer in silence.

"Nothing unusual yet, unless Larby turns out to be Landesman. Let's see if Larby's car is here first."

They all walked up toward the trailer together. As they passed more of the trailers and RVs, Crista was aware of several people peering at them from behind shaded windows. It was strange that there was no one around. Was everyone afraid of something? Well, she reasoned, Jose Traviso hadn't been. But it was amazingly quiet for a circus camp. Weren't circuses supposed to be fun?

They came up alongside the RV with three poodles on the side. Jeff walked around on the other side. While Crista and Steve surveyed the RV, getting down the license plate and a basic description, Jeff came back along the side. "What did you say the license plate was?"

Steve told him.

Jeff said, "Yup, it's over there behind the RV."

Everyone rushed around and there sat the white station wagon Steve remembered that the Landesman character had driven. They looked inside the car, but it was locked. A second later, they heard a branch snap.

Turning around, they all gaped at a gray-haired woman with a double-barreled shotgun in her arms. "What're ya doin' here, you three?" she said and raised the gun till it was aimed right at Steve Leonard's chest.

·13·

The Poodles

"We're looking for Jon Larby," Steve said right away, not looking as afraid as Crista thought he must have been.

The woman lowered the gun. "What do you want with him?"

"Just to ask a few questions. About the escaped bear."

"He don't know nothin' about it," she said, turning and opening the breech of the shotgun and pulling out the shells. "He's with the dogs right now."

"Can we go talk to him?"

"Sure, he's over with them by the swimming pool, which isn't filled. It makes a nice staging area."

Crista, Jeff, and Steve walked over behind the motel. As they came around a corner, they heard yapping. A moment later, they saw the six poodles performing on the apron of the pool. A tall, leggy man held up a hoop that the dogs jumped through, first singly and then in pairs and finally in two trios. The threesome watched for a minute, taking in what must have been part of the usual dog show with the circus. He was in the process of getting the poodles to perform a dog-on-dog pyramid, much like acrobats occasionally did. Crista had done the same maneuver in gym at school.

"Hey, there!" Steve called. "You Jon Larby?"

The tall man turned around. He looked younger than Crista had imagined, especially since the bear trainer, Cal Turner, had looked so old. Steve walked across the concrete, extending his hand. Crista and Jeff shuffled after him.

"I'm Steve Leonard from the local paper," Steve said. "Just wanted to ask a few questions."

"Sure," Jon Larby replied, turning back to the dogs. "Rollovers, everyone. Three."

Immediately, each of the dogs began doing rollovers in a line, all of them in perfect unison like pairs of skaters performing duets on ice. They did three rollovers, then stopped suddenly, all of them, on their feet after the third one. It was really a marvel to watch. They accomplished it with a precision Crista knew was unusual.

"Just some questions about the circus," Steve said. Crista watched as he pulled out his notebook. "How long have you been with them?"

"Seven, no, eight years this season."

"Been with any other circuses?"

"Two." Larby had thin, almost haggard features and Steve gave no indication whether he was the same man who had appeared making the claim about the bear mauling. "Ringling Brothers—they didn't pay enough. And before that, 'The Big Top,' which was a total bust."

"So you like the Halloran Brothers?"

"They're all right. You sent by my boss or something? Well, tell them I like them real well. Real well. They're good to me, and I feel fine about the whole arrangement."

"That's great," Steve said. Crista wondered why he didn't ask any questions about the mauling. But it was plain, if this man had been involved, he clearly wasn't the one mauled. There wasn't a mark on him. His hollow cheeks were all clean and smooth, completely free of razor burn let alone a swat from a grizzly bear.

Steve went on, "What kind of tricks do your dogs do?"

"You name it. Everything. They're well trained. I've been a trainer ever since a boy. My dad and mom were with the circus before me." The man seemed friendly, certainly not hostile. He didn't act like he was hiding anything.

"Can you show us some?" Steve turned to Crista. "Want to take some pictures?"

Crista was taken aback. "Some pictures?"

"Sure. For the paper, for the story."

As Larby set up, Crista whispered, "What story? What are you doing?"

"Just watch," Steve answered, low and crisp.

"Is it him?" Jeff asked.

"It fits," Steve said under his breath. That was all he would volunteer. "Now get that camera flicking."

Crista began shooting as the dogs performed a number of moves with the hoop. In one trick, the two black dogs held the hoop in their teeth while the other four jumped through. Next, the dogs rolled several hoops along by pushing with their noses. Then one balanced a hoop—only one of the dogs did this—on his nose. Crista got a picture of everything. Mr. Larby commented as the dogs did the routine, giving them directions and orders at various points.

"They're really good," Steve said.

Mr. Larby rounded up the dogs. "Do you need any more material?"

"No, this is enough. I just hope it doesn't get in the way of the bear story."

"Bear story?" Mr. Larby said, dropping his jaw. Crista could see he was really disappointed.

"Oh, you know, this big thing about the escaped grizzly and him mauling someone and the other two bears. I guess they're a big act with the circus, even though it doesn't look that big to me."

Larby shook his head. "These dogs outshow those bears every time. All they do is a little circling around and Turner sits on the shoulders of one—the one that escaped—and they do some somersaults and people think they've just won All Circus. It makes me mad."

"Yeah," Steve said. "And that guy who owns them? What an old barf-brain he is!"

"You got that right," Larby replied. Crista watched with amazement as Steve led Larby on, getting all the information he wanted. "Turner is an old dope who needs to get out of the business. His bears are passé. They're not even ferocious, though I wouldn't put it past them to maul someone. Undisciplined is what they are. That makes them dangerous. He doesn't keep them under control the way he should. Why, one time in the ring, the big one went after little Alfie, my best poodle. Almost got the poor boy in his teeth, except my other dogs surrounded the big lug and confused him. Turner said the dogs distracted his act. Well, it was none of that at all."

"I didn't know about that," Steve said, writing. "Why is it that Halloran favors the bear act over the dogs?"

"I never got it." Larby shook his head. "Halloran likes the danger of it, I guess. Same as the lions. He thinks it gets people's blood flowing. But my doggies should get much better billing than they do."

"I'll see if I can put in a good word," Steve said, shaking Larby's hand. "By the way, you ought to tell your missus not to be running around with a shotgun. She's going to scare someone."

"Ah, she's a cream puff," Larby said, smiling. "My boys are the real gunslingers."

"Your boys?" Steve asked. Crista swallowed, praying momentarily that they were both holed up in the trailer sleeping late or something.

"Yeah, they're out on the trail, looking for the bear. They're real good shots, and if that bear causes any trouble, neither of them will hesitate to use their guns, I assure you of that."

"Your boys are out there?" Steve looked unhappily at Crista and Jeff.

"So are a lot of other circus people. That bear's a real menace. Hurt people in the ring several times, but Halloran covered it up. No love lost between a lot of folks around here and that Turner and his three bears. But I really don't want to see the bear hurt, understand. It's just that he is a problem. I'm sure someone is bound to get hurt real bad."

"Somebody already was," Steve said.

Larby acted as if he knew nothing. "Oh, really?"

"Somebody named Landesman came into the news office a couple nights ago. Reported to the police that he was mauled by the bear at the dump. Pretty bad case, I think."

"Well, there you go." Larby smiled toothily, his cigarette smoker's teeth yellowed at the cracks.

"Thanks for your time, sir."

"Anytime," Larby said, turning back to the dogs and telling them to line up.

Steve, Crista, and Jeff walked off toward Steve's car. When they were out of hearing distance, around the edge of the motel, Steve said, "Well, now we have a motive."

"We do?" Jeff asked. "All you did was tell him what a great act he had."

"Yeah, but you weren't listening," Crista said, frowning. "Pretty smart, Steve. He didn't even know you were finding out about circus-act relations. He thought you were on his side and just making talk."

"Exactly," Steve said. "So what did we find out?"

"That he doesn't think much of the bear act," Crista replied.

Jeff's face had a quizzical look plastered all over it, when suddenly he appeared to get it. "Oh, I see!" His face brightened. "And he probably thinks they should be dumped. So now was his chance."

"Precisely," Steve said. "So now we go to plan B."

"What's that?" Crista asked.

"I don't know yet," Steve answered. Crista laughed. Jeff still seemed lost in getting the previous story. Steve continued, "But we're on the way. I think he's the one. The person who came by the other night was tall and slim. And that definitely was the car. So we can try and see if there's anyone else who fits the description. But I'm sure it was Larby."

"Meanwhile, what about Vic? And Mr. Turner?" Crista said. "Mr. Larby's two sons are out there, probably on orders from him to kill the bear if they can."

"Yeah, I think we'd better find out what's with the Sheriff of Nottingham and his Merry Men."

"Wasn't that Robin Hood?" Jeff asked.

"Whatever," Steve said.

Crista decided she liked Steve now. He wasn't as arrogant as she'd originally thought, and he could be downright shrewd, too.

·14·

The Sheriff's Merry Men

Steve barreled down the road to where the police and the others had parked their cars to gather together to capture the bear. There were two men with rifles on guard at the edge of the woods. Steve parked on the opposite side of the road and waited. "Well, what should we do?" he finally asked.

"Shouldn't we tell them what we know?" Crista answered.

"Yeah, but I don't know what good it would do. They're loaded literally for bear."

"But we have to try," Crista said, hitting her fist on the dashboard.

"I agree," Jeff said. "What if they just shoot him when they don't have to?"

"All right," Steve said. "Let's walk over and find out what's happening. Then we can figure out where to go from here."

The three walked across the road and over to one of the men lolling against a tree, a shotgun slung across his left arm in hunting fashion. He was an officer from town. Crista recognized him as one of the men who had driven a snowmobile months before when Nadine Semms had been rescued while in labor with her babies.

Steve introduced himself. Crista noticed that the officer's little nameplate above his left pocket said Detective Marlboro.

"Read your articles," the policeman said to Steve, not offering a hand. "Pretty good stuff."

"Well, I have more," Steve said. "You know about this so-called mauling incident?"

"Of course."

"It might be a setup." Steve looked from Jeff to Crista and said, "These two kids were in a cabin back in the woods last night when the bear showed up. They say the bear didn't attack them, didn't even act unfriendly. In fact, he stood out in the yard and danced in the moonlight."

The policeman grinned. "This keeps getting better all the time. Now he's a dancing grizzly. Well, I, for one, am not going around the critter without some weaponry in my hand."

"Look," Crista broke in. "You have to understand. The bear's practically tame. And he didn't maul that man, either. We think he's from the circus and is jealous of the bear act. He's trying to destroy it."

"Right," Steve added. "The man who claimed to be mauled is really a person named Jon Larby who runs the dog show for the circus. Apparently, he and Cal Turner, the man who does the bear show, are on the outs, and Larby is trying to eliminate the bear show so he can be number one."

"Circus politics, huh?"

"Yeah," Steve said. "But the bear is virtually harmless. If they shoot him, it's on false pretenses."

The officer laughed. "I know you're concerned about the bear and all. But it's still a very dangerous animal. I assure you, everything is being done to preserve him as best as possible. So just hang tough and let us do our work."

"Yeah, but there are a lot of circus people out there, too, right?" Steve asked.

"Best ones to help," Marlboro said. "They know the bear and how to handle him. Except the guy who owns them. Real fruitcake, that guy."

"He is not!" Crista cried. "He's a very decent man."

"Yeah, but he's in love with his bears."

"If you're going to be part of a show like that, maybe that's the best way to be," Steve replied.

"And two of those people out there are Mr. Larby's sons," Crista added. "Don't you see, they want to shoot the bear and get rid of him?"

"That's not my job, I'm sorry to say," the officer said. "Now just move back away from the cars and get across the road. We don't want any people hurt in this matter."

"But the bear hasn't done anything except escape," Crista said evenly.

The officer shook his head firmly. "I'm sorry, but that's not the point here. The animal is dangerous. But if it's any comfort to you, Mr. Turner is out there with a stun gun and other equipment. Not that I think he can pull it off. Guy can barely walk straight. But I assure you, they want to bring that bear in alive."

"Not all of them," Crista murmured.

"I'm sorry. You'll just have to talk to the sheriff," Marlboro answered a final time, then turned to another officer standing nearby and looked at his watch. "When are they coming back in?"

"Hour and a half or so."

He looked back at Steve. "They should be back pretty soon. They're supposed to be back within an hour and a half unless they spot the bear. Then they'll keep going."

"Thanks. Come on," Steve said. He wheeled Crista around, gave her a stern look, and pointed to the car.

As they walked away from the police officer, Crista said, "I don't think it really matters what we say. We're just kids."

"Don't worry," Steve said. "I just figured out what plan B is."

"What?"

"We go back to the trailers and see if we can find the bandages Larby used to pull off his hoax. If we find them, we have a stronger case and maybe they'll believe we're right."

"Good idea," Jeff said.

Crista nodded. "All right. And maybe we should be prepared for other things."

"Like what?"

"Like a hungry bear, for one thing. Let's stop at the store and pick up several packages of hot dogs. Hopefully Vic is hungry enough to eat the hot dogs, but not hungry enough to eat us."

Steve laughed. "I suppose I have to pay for it, too."

"Reporter's expense," Crista said.

"All right," Steve replied, "but this better be good."

"One other thing," Crista added. "I think you need to meet Nadine, too. And Johnny Junior. He was sick last night, and I want to find out how he is. And maybe you can write a story about them. It's pretty dramatic, if you ask me. It was at their house that we saw the bear."

Steve nodded. "We'll go after we get the hot dogs and go by the trailer park."

They stopped at Al's Grocery at the top of the hill, and Steve paid for three dozen hot dogs rather reluctantly. Crista assured him it would be for a good cause. Then they sped back to the trailer park to check out what trash was available, but they found all the cans were empty.

"They must have collected it this morning," Crista sighed

"So where do they take it?" Steve asked.

Crista and Jeff knew the answer to that one. "The dump!"

"But that's huge!" Steve said.

They all stopped at the motel office to ask.

"That Mr. Clemmons, the dump guy, has it all organized," the man in the motel office told them. "He makes our truck put it in one place. Each truck has a special place. What do you want to see the garbage for?"

"We're collectors," Steve said on the way out.

"There's tons and tons of it anyway." Crista was feeling discouraged. "And there're rats there, and bugs. More bugs that you've ever seen in your life."

"Look, do you want to save a bear or not?" Steve asked. "This was your idea, by the way!"

Nodding reluctantly, Crista said, "But I didn't know it would mean going through garbage."

"What do you think the bear's been doing?" Steve said.

On the way to the dump, Steve went by Nadine's on the back roads. Johnny was at work, but Nadine set Cokes around for all, and they talked about the bear and the kids.

"I haven't seen him," Nadine said. "But the woods tend to get quiet all of a sudden sometimes, as if something big and horrible is passing by. Sometimes when I'm putting out the wash, I hear it. It kind of gives me the creeps."

"But you haven't actually seen him?" Steve asked.

"I'm not making a date, if that's what you mean," Nadine answered. Crista picked up Johnny Junior and showed Steve and Jeff the little lump on his belly where his small intestine had broken through the muscle wall.

"Yeah, it looks bad," Nadine admitted. "We took him in this morning, and the doctor says they'll have to go ahead with the operation as soon as possible. He doesn't like Junior throwing up the way he was last night."

"That's why we're here," Crista said. "Steve might be able to help."

"I don't want any charity," Nadine was quick to reply. "We've got to make our own way."

"I understand that," Steve said. "But we could do an article about it. It wouldn't be charity if some people decided to help you out."

"Well," Nadine looked uncomfortably at Crista and Jeff. Crista swung Johnny Junior back and forth in her arms, and the tiny boy smiled and gurgled. Nadine said, "I don't like owing people, but I guess in this day and age I'll have to be more humble about it."

"And maybe it would be God's way of helping you, Nay," Crista said, then cooed to the baby and laughed.

"Yeah, I can't argue with that." Nadine picked up Fairlight. "I think God's been taking good care of us, but I have been wondering how He would fix this problem."

Steve stood. "I'll see if I can get something going." He touched Johnny's head gently, then turned to Crista and Jeff. "We need to get on to the dump."

"Right," Crista said. She set Johnny Junior down on the couch and gave Nadine a hug and then each of the twins a kiss. "Pray for us," she said. "We're on a real detective mission."

"Be careful," Nadine said.

They were off.

·15·

In the Dump

"Yeah, they just dumped it this morning," Mr. Clemmons said. He was a short, skinny man, very wrinkled and old-looking, and had been at the dump for years. No one remembered when he hadn't been at the dump. "I have it all worked out. Motels over here—" he pointed to one of the easier access areas. "Residents on the lake over here." He marched over and showed them a long overhang with railroad ties marking off the edges. Flies zoomed through the air in legions. Crista didn't see any rats, but she could feel their presence. It made her skin crawl to think of opening some trash bag and finding a family of little rats feasting on some thrown-out hamburger or pork chop.

"And tourists over here." He showed the most difficult access spot of all, right out in the middle of the debris. "I like to make them work. Then they won't come back as often."

Crista knew about the area's particular dislike of tourists, even though they were responsible for most of the money that came into the region.

"Right," Steve said. "Well, we're not tourists, and we need to find something very important to save a life."

"Oh yeah, whose?" Mr. Clemmons asked, leaning on a pitchfork.

111

"Vic's."

Mr. Clemmons nodded. "Whoever he is, I hope you find it." He turned back to his work, which was shoveling trash in the residential area into the fire that wafted black smoke into the air and gave the dump a nasty, rotten garbage smell. The dump area itself was a large bowl. They stood on the close side, but it reached across a good two hundred feet. The bowl was less than a quarter filled up.

"Let's get going," Steve said, walking over to the edge of the motel area and looking over. "This is gonna take awhile."

"Do we really have to do this?" Crista asked. "Wouldn't it be better just to go tell the sheriff what we saw and heard?"

"But what evidence do we have that will really stick?" Jeff said. He was already tying a bandanna around his head. Crista could tell he liked the idea of jumping in the bundles of trash and groping around. Who knew what a boy could find to take home and set up on his shelf? The dump, Johnny Semms had often said, "was the best department store on the East Coast, and it didn't cost anything."

"Yuck!" Crista yelled, as she gingerly stepped over to one of the plastic white bags that had once been the liner of a trash can. "How do we even know any of this is from the motel?"

"You can tell," Steve said. "The trash'll probably have things in it to identify where it's from. Maybe fliers or brochures or a piece of paper with a letterhead on it. There are all kinds of ways."

Crista opened one of the bags. Flies and innumerable other bugs bombed around like they were in trash heaven. It seemed like she could even hear them shouting to one another: "Hey, Rudy! Over here! I found a great lamb chop with some meat on it!" "Yo, Harry. Look at this: a whole pile of peas and onions with gravy mixed in. I dreamed about this last night!"

"Gross," Crista murmured to herself as she peered into the bag. It was mostly food and she didn't have to look long to realize this wasn't the one she was looking for. She thought Vic might enjoy it, though. Down at the bottom of the dump, she saw several of the dump dogs nosing around in the trash, too. Rontu and Tigger had once been dump dogs. But they were Crista's now and didn't need to pick trash to survive. Crista felt sorry for the dump dogs. They were all scraggly, ugly-looking creatures, dirty and always ready for a fight. She wondered if any of them had seen the bear and been afraid, or if the bear had played with them like he had with Mr. Turner's old dog, Sylvester.

She knew, though, not to go near the dogs. Most of them were vicious, and who knew what diseases they carried? She ignored them for now. She just hoped they didn't bother the bear.

Jeff strode into the middle of the pile and began throwing bags and articles left and right. He found a bag of old clothes that someone had chucked. A broken chair. A whole sink with chips and nicks all over it. Broken pieces of wood.

Then suddenly Steve called out. "Hey, here's some pictures of people at the circus. We're getting close."

Jeff waded over to where Steve was, knee-deep in grunge and green plastic bags. Crista balanced herself on top of one of the piles and looked for a way over to where they were standing. Steve rifled through the bags quickly, spilling their contents all over and peering through them.

"Well, I guess I just have to do what I can do," Crista said, heaving up another green plastic yard bag and dumping it out. Dirty napkins and greasy plates with ketchup and mustard stains on them sloshed out. Jeff picked up one of the plates and, with a flick of his wrist, set it sailing off over the dump like a Frisbee.

"Hey, we could really have some fun here," he said jovially.

Crista picked up a paper plate and threw it. "Mine went farther," she said to Jeff.

"Oh yeah? Watch this!" With a mighty heave, Jeff sent another paper plate sailing over the dump.

"You think you're so tough," Crista laughed. "My grandmother throws better than that!"

"Oh yeah? We'll see about that!"

"Hey!" Steve interrupted. "This is important. Quit messing around!"

"Okay, okay," Crista said, getting back to business and sifting through the next garbage bag. It was more picnic items, but there were also some overexposed Polaroid pictures that had been torn up. Crista picked them up and scrutinized them for a moment, but there was no one from the circus or anywhere else that she recognized.

"This is hopeless!" she burst out. "We'll never find those things! And what makes us so sure he didn't burn the bandages or something? How do we even know he threw it into the trash?"

"First rule of investigative reporting," Steve said. "Check out the trash. It tells a lot about the people you're investigating, whether you know it or not."

"Like what?" Crista stopped and stared at him. Her camera hung over her neck and bounced against her chest as she stood up to look through one more bag of gooey napkins and plates.

Steve stepped back from a bag and gained his balance. "Like these photographs. Who knows what they might show if you have the right trash? Or some special papers or letters or something. People throw away those things all the time. And they figure no one will ever find it because it's trash and just too much of it. But people do."

"Then shouldn't we be careful what we touch?" Crista said, wiping her brow. In the warm air, she was sweating now. It was still cold out, about fifty degrees or so, but with the fires billowing up smoke just thirty yards away it was far warmer than normal. "We don't want to mess up fingerprints or anything like that, do we?"

Steve shook his head. "Yeah, I never thought of that. Wait a second!" He rushed over the bags, stumbling and pitching around like he would fall down, then reached hard ground. "I have several pairs of winter gloves in the trunk that I keep there in case I get stuck in a snowdrift or something. Some gardening gloves, too. That'll keep us from getting fingerprints on anything. Sorry I didn't think of it earlier!"

"Great!" Crista murmured sarcastically. "It's a good thing we all know what we're doing here!"

"Yo! Look at this!" Jeff suddenly said.

Everyone turned around.

"What is it?" Steve called.

"Three lug nuts!"

"Don't touch them!" Steve yelled.

Crista walked over and looked down into the bag. There were three lug nuts, the kinds of nuts that were used to hold a tire to a hub on a truck or car or trailer.

"Why would someone throw away that?" Crista asked.

"Don't you remember?" Steve said, walking across the piles. "The way Daring Dan's trailer broke up— one of the rear tires was missing some lug nuts!"

He handed Crista and Jeff each a pair of work gloves, and he put on a pair of ski mittens.

"Pick them up and put them in this bag," Steve said, handing Jeff a brown supermarket bag.

Everyone stood over the bag, looking through it as Jeff pulled out first one then another article.

"Whoa!" Jeff suddenly said. "Look at this!"

Jeff pulled out a length of gauze and Ace bandage. It dangled from his hand like a limp snake. It was more than enough to make the head bandage that Steve said Landesman had come to him with. He also found several pieces of tape.

"This could be Larby's own trash bag," Steve said excitedly. "What else is in there?"

All three of them stooped down and poured out the contents of the trash bag. There were several expended shotgun shells, a couple of tools—a bent screwdriver and a pair of pliers that had broken in half—and more bandages.

"This ought to be more than enough to nail this guy," Steve said excitedly. "This is tremendous."

Jeff and Crista gathered the items into the brown grocery bag and started back toward the car.

"Anything else we need?" she asked as Steve put the bag in his trunk and took off the gloves. "Anyone for a broken cocktail glass? And I saw a good half of a hamburger back that way. Jeff, you hungry?"

"Don't make jokes," Steve said. "This is serious."

"How do we know any of this belongs to Jon Larby anyway?" she asked.

"We don't. But the police may be able to find out," Steve said. "Through fingerprinting and so on. It's a chance we'll have to take. But it all makes sense, doesn't it? All the evidence in one place. He obviously threw it all away together. I doubt anyone else would be throwing away lug nuts like that."

"Okay," Crista said. "But I'm not sure anyone will believe us."

"That's a chance we'll have to take," Steve admitted. "I thought you wanted to save Vic."

"I do," Crista said. "But I feel kind of hopeless at the moment."

"Don't feel that way!" Steve cried. "We have the goods!"

Crista smiled at Steve's sudden exuberance. He rarely showed his light side. He started to shut the trunk where he had put the evidence when there was a boom in the distance. Everyone stopped immediately and listened. There were two more quick booms in the air, then all was silent.

"Guns!" Crista exclaimed with fear.

"We've got to hurry," Steve said. "They might have him cornered."

"But what are we going to do?" Jeff broke in. "They won't let us go up on the mountain, and if they've got the bear now, what can we do?"

"Mr. Belfield!" Crista suddenly shouted. "Let's go get Mr. Belfield! Maybe he would know where to go, what to do to track the bear—if he's even still alive."

"Who's Mr. Belfield?" Steve asked.

"Some old hunter," Jeff said with a smile.

"He's a nice man!" Crista insisted. "And he is a hunter." She had told Jeff about Mr. Belfield's story. "And he'll know what to do to find the bear, too, or at least to get him out of danger."

"All right, let's go," Steve said, opening the car door.

Mr. Clemmons walked over with his pitchfork as Jeff and Crista opened the doors on the other side of the car. "Find what you were lookin' for?" he asked.

"More than we were looking for," Crista said, smiling.

"Sounds like they're getting that bear put away," Mr. Clemmons said. "You hear the gunfire?"

"Yes," Crista said.

Jeff suddenly said to Mr. Clemmons, "If you see them—the sheriff or any of the others—tell them we have evidence that the bear didn't do what they say he did."

"You do, huh?" Mr. Clemmons said. "He was here, you know. Several times."

"How do you know?"

"Found his poops!"

Steve laughed in the car and Mr. Clemmons said, "I don't think he's a bad bear anyway. Didn't mess things up around here too much. So I'd give him the time of day."

Crista jumped into the car. "Let's go. There isn't much time—if we haven't run out already."

Steve wheeled out of the yard, leaving a spray of dust and leaves as he propelled the car out of the parking lot.

"We can go the back way," Crista said. "Hurry!"

·16·

Ideas and Actions

Mr. Belfield wore a bright red shirt and overalls. He had been working on one of the windows, caulking it. He stepped down off the ladder when Steve pulled into the yard. Crista breathlessly poured out the story. Mr. Belfield said, "You want to catch a bear, you have to lure him with what he likes."

"We have a bunch of hot dogs," Crista said.

"That'll do it. Nothing like a wienie roast to bring out all the grizzlies in the woods."

They all waited as Mr. Belfield went inside and then came back out dressed in a hunting jacket and holding a large pistol. "I don't intend to use this, but whether this bear is dangerous or not is yet to be seen. Now we have to stick together and I'll drive my truck. No need for that little toy you got there, Mr. Leonard."

"Would it be better to ride?" Crista asked. "Horses, I mean?" The moment she said it, she remembered that first scene when Val the bear stood up in front of her and Betsarama. No, they didn't need horses. Betsarama was probably having nightmares about that episode!

"No, the horses might get spooked," Mr. Belfield replied. "I'm sure Wilkins would let us use the horses, but if they got scared, who knows what would happen?

We could end up on the wrong side of a stampede, someone could get thrown or trampled, anything could happen. No, my truck is best and safest. Got plenty of gas and a grizzly would more likely run from a truck than confront it."

They all climbed into Mr. Belfield's double cab, double rear-tire truck. He said it could go through anything and it looked like it. He started it up and then gave everyone a hard look. "Got the hot dogs?"

"Yup!"

"Got the gun?"

"Yup!"

"Got the guts?"

There was a pause. Then Crista and Jeff said, "Yup!" Steve, however, looked a little green. Mr. Belfield was just about to pull down the driveway and drive to the main road, when a little figure appeared running up the driveway toward them.

"It's Lindy!" Crista yelled.

Lindy sprinted up out of breath, her freckled face red with exhaustion. "It was on the news," she cried between breaths. "They got the bear up at the top of the mountain, and two of the men took shots. But they missed and the bear escaped!"

"Thank the Lord for that," Mr. Belfield said. "Are you coming, too?"

Crista opened the back door.

"Wait a second," Mr. Belfield said. "Do your parents all know where you are? This is dangerous business here, and I probably shouldn't let any of you out of the truck up there. There's men with guns out there. I'm not sure this is such a good idea, kids."

"I talked to my dad," Crista said immediately, "and he said it was okay for me to go with Steve. Jeff's grandmother says it's okay too."

"What about Lindy here?"

"I told my mother I saw a car go up your driveway. But I guess we'd better stop and ask." She gave Crista and then Mr. Belfield a look of distress. Crista knew the last thing they could do now was leave Lindy behind.

"All right," Mr. Belfield said. "Now, Steve. Is it okay with your mom?"

Steve laughed and everyone laughed with him. "Yeah, I have a special pass from her to go into any danger that will get a good story or get me bumped off. She never liked me too much. And all the insurance goes to her anyway."

Mr. Belfield laughed. "All right, Lindy," he said. "It's up to you. But none of you kids are getting out of this truck, understand?"

There was a reluctant, "All right." Mr. Belfield hit the gas and turned onto the back road toward the Helstroms' place. He stopped at Lindy's house and gave Lindy two minutes to run inside. Mrs. Helstrom came out, mopping her brow.

"Baking pies today," she said. "What's this about Lindy and Crista and all you going up on the mountain?"

"Just trying to help out," Mr. Belfield said. "The kids here are concerned that someone is trying to get the bear shot, and I think the sheriff should hear the story. I'm not letting any of them out of the truck, though, if that's what you're worried about. I know a bear's dangerous, tame or not. And there are a lot of men walking around up there who are a mite trigger-happy, so I'm not going to let them get into any danger. We're just going to try to talk to the sheriff."

"Well, all right, as long as Lindy promises not to get out of the truck—at all. Hear that, little girl? You are to obey Mr. Belfield and Crista, you understand that? No getting out of this truck."

"Of course, Mom. I'll do everything they say."

Crista smiled. "Get on all fours and roll over, then."

Lindy fell to the ground, but Crista grabbed her at the collar. "Just a joke."

"I'll watch out for her," she said to Mrs. Helstrom. "And none of us are getting out of the truck unless it topples over and bursts into flames."

Everyone turned to look at her with wonder and exasperation.

"Just looking on the bright side," she said, and then punched Jeff in the arm. "It's okay. You can laugh." She felt much better now that Mr. Belfield was with them. He made her feel very confident. He had to be one of the bravest people she ever met.

Mr. Belfield turned back to Mrs. Helstrom. "I'll watch out for them. They are not going to get within a mile of any danger, I assure you."

"Okay, have a good time. And save that bear. Even I think that at this point!"

Mr. Belfield started down the road toward the cutoff that veered back to the Semms' cabin and the dump, and then came out on the other side of the mountain. He said, "There's a trail we can follow, I think the truck'll make it, but we'll have to be careful."

"There's an old road, too," Lindy said. "Remember when Lukas went crazy and ran down it, Crista?"

"Could I ever forget that?" Crista explained to Mr. Belfield and Steve how she and Jeff taught Lindy to ride the Wilkinses' horses. One time, though, Lukas went a little crazy or something and took off down the old electric company road into the trees. It was a miracle that Crista and a friend named Cruz had been able to save Lindy from falling off the horse as he careened along at forty miles an hour.

Mr. Belfield said, "We can catch that on the other side of the Semms' cabin. But for now, we need to go slow and keep our bearings. Our mission is to find the sheriff and tell him what you all have discovered. That should get the heat off this bear so that they capture him and don't kill him. Is everyone agreed on that? I don't want any of you suddenly acting like a hero."

"Oh, rats, and I thought this was my big chance," Jeff said. The tension faded as everyone looked to Mr. Belfield to make things right.

"We have it," Steve said, looking around at the others. "This'll be the greatest story I ever had, and it's only my first week on the job!"

"The sheriff, ladies and gentlemen," Mr. Belfield reminded them. "Keep your eyes on red alert for the sheriff."

They barnstormed up the hill on the dirt road toward the dump. When they reached the T in the road—left to the dump, right to the Semms' cabin and the road up the mountain—Mr. Belfield stopped and tapped his fingers on the steering wheel. "If they're up on the mountain and they cornered the bear, we have to figure out which way the bear would go so we can catch up to the men. Would he go toward the dump, or down the mountain to places he's familiar with where he might have a hideout?"

"He must know the dump is death by now," Jeff said.

"And maybe that's why he came out to the Semms' cabin—twice that we know of," Crista exclaimed. "Maybe that's where his hideout is—somewhere there in the trees."

"Good thinking, kids," Mr. Belfield said. "Then we should warn your friends that the grizzly might be coming."

"Good idea," Crista said, glad to have one more chance to check on Nadine and make sure Johnny was there.

Mr. Belfield turned the truck to the right and stomped on the gas pedal. Dust and dirt splattered out behind them as they rattled up the road, a shovel, pick, and other garden implements jostling around in the bed of the truck in the back. Crista noticed for the first time that the truck had a sunroof like many cars, and it was equipped with a CB radio, another radio which she didn't recognize, and a gun rack across the back window—with no guns, fortunately. The back window could be opened, too. She noticed seal clips on either side of it.

They drove down the road at thirty-five miles an hour. Everyone kept a lookout on both sides with the windows down, listening for the sound of any gunfire or a sight of the sheriff and his men or the bear. No one saw anything. They soon pulled into the yard behind the Semms' cabin. As Mr. Belfield stopped the truck, Johnny ran out and a moment later Nadine followed with both twins in her arms. He rushed over to Mr. Belfield's window and said, "What's up? You look like you're on the way to a fire."

"Almost," Mr. Belfield said, holding out his hand. "I'm Frank Belfield, neighbor of the Wilkinses and the Helstroms. You know Crista and Jeff, I guess." He introduced Steve Leonard, and Steve shook hands with Johnny. They made quite a contrast. Johnny was tall—about six-three or four, Crista thought—lanky, gangly, and dark, and Steve was short, a little pudgy, red-faced, and light-skinned. For a moment, Crista thought of how you make so many different kinds of friends in life, and each can be so different from the other. Yet, they can still become beloved friends— both with you and with one another.

"We've been listening to the radio," Johnny said. "Turn it on. They're really tracking the bear. But it got away about fifteen minutes ago."

"We think he's coming here," Crista said.

Johnny looked thunderstruck and Nadine turned white. "Here?" she asked, her voice almost a squeak.

"Yup!" Jeff said. "We think his hideout is somewhere around here. That's why he was around all those times."

Nadine's eyes opened wide. "You know, Johnny and I have been convinced he's been around."

"Maybe he's been watching out for the twins," Lindy volunteered. "Until they ripen and are ready to eat."

Everyone laughed, but Nadine gave Lindy a sour look.

"Really," Crista said. "We're convinced he may be heading back here to get to his hideout before they capture him. He really wants to be on his own and doesn't want to be caught."

"Then let's get into the cabin, Johnny. And load the gun," Nadine added.

"You don't mind if we take a gander up the trail, do you?" Mr. Belfield said. "We want to get to the sheriff before he gets to the bear."

"Be my guest," Johnny said. Nadine was already walking back to the cabin with the twins in her arms. He looked after her, then grinned. "Got to protect the wife, if you know what I mean."

"Yeah, right," Lindy teased. "Probably be in there kissing instead of protecting!"

"Lindy!" Crista and Jeff exclaimed together.

"She's the resident comedian, I see," Steve remarked.

Mr. Belfield jammed the shifter into gear. He backed out toward the sliver of road leading into the woods.

"The road goes right up to the top of the mountain," Crista said. "I've used it lots of times. It's steep in places."

"This truck don't mind steepness," Mr. Belfield said, his goatee sticking out like a briar patch.

Crista focused her camera, trying to get it ready for action. Lindy cracked jokes to Jeff, while Jeff stared out the window, probably wishing he had a gun, too—or so Crista figured. To use on Lindy, if nothing else! They drove about a hundred yards in, then Mr. Belfield suddenly stopped.

"What's the matter?" Steve said. He was in the front seat next to Mr. Belfield.

"Look up there in the road."

Everyone peered straight ahead, but saw nothing.

"I'm getting out for a minute," Mr. Belfield said. "You all just wait here."

He clambered out of the left door of the truck and stood for a moment listening. He didn't close the door. Crista, Lindy, and Jeff leaned forward over the back of the front seat and Steve leaned forward, shielding his eyes. The tension cranked back to extremely high, and everyone seemed on edge. Had Mr. Belfield seen the bear? If he had, why would he get out?

"If the bear smells the hot dogs, he may try to get in here, you know," Lindy suddenly said.

"Great, bringing that up now," Crista answered.

"Well, if he wants either a hot dog or Jeff, I'm giving him whichever he wants first."

"Thanks a lot," Jeff huffed.

Mr. Belfield stooped at a point up the road, about twenty feet in front of the truck. He picked up a stick and began swishing it in front of him.

"What's he doing?" Jeff whispered.

"Digging a hole?" Steve guessed.

"No," Lindy answered. "He's making a wish."

"Oh, yeah, what kind of wish?" Crista asked. She was feeling nervous and edgy, wishing Mr. Belfield would come back. Even though she didn't want the bear to be harmed, she still felt afraid of it. And with the door open, it could climb right in and give everyone a big bite.

"A wish that the bear would come out of the woods and . . ." Lindy looked around, then poked Crista in the side.

"Yipes!"

"Just like that," Lindy said, smiling.

"You are a little pain!" Crista yelled and grabbed Lindy around the shoulders and shook her.

"That's what my mom says!" Lindy said triumphantly.

"You're all nuts," Jeff commented.

Steve said, "I think it's a bear flop."

"A what?" Lindy asked.

"Doo-doo. You know. The bear pooped in the road," Steve said. "Good grief, do I have to make it any plainer?"

Everyone looked ahead again as Mr. Belfield stood. He held up a Kleenex and let it stretch out in the breeze. Then he walked back to the truck.

"It's a pattie," he said. "Bear went right in the road. It's recent, too. Maybe a half day old. And it has some little bones in it. Bear's been eating a lot of garbage, maybe even catching his own prey. Don't know about that yet."

"You can tell all that from the pattie?" Crista asked. She leaned forward and tried to focus in on it, but it was not clear on her viewfinder. There was no point in taking a picture when you couldn't even tell what it was that you were looking at.

"You sure can," Mr. Belfield replied. He jumped back into the truck and sat in the seat, thinking. "We could be in trouble though. We're upwind from the mountain. Bear'll smell us and he'll either veer off somewhere else, or else he'll turn around and head right back into the sheriff's guns. Something may help, though."

"What's that?" Steve asked.

"I'm going to put the pattie right on the hood of the truck!"

"Oh, gross."

"Yuck."

"You're going to do what?"

"Pick up the bear flop and lay it on the hood of the truck," Mr. Belfield said again. He grinned. "It may conceal our smell a bit, and if we keep the windows closed it won't be too bad. Bears have an incredible sense of smell, though—*acute* is the word. They're the best nosers in the wilderness, so it probably won't do a lot of good by way of camouflage. It may make him curious, though."

"Do we really have to do this?" Crista said, her stomach turning over at the idea.

"Heck, I've covered my whole getup in bear flop at times, just to bag one," Mr. Belfield said with a laugh. "This is nothin'! Anyway, bear flop isn't so bad. He turned around and smiled. Crista smelled the pipe smoke on his breath, but it was a pleasant, aromatic scent and she didn't mind it.

"Well, we're all keeping our windows closed," Jeff said, "so I guess it's okay."

Mr. Belfield got out again and closed his door. Crista, though, wanted to get some pictures again. "Come on, Steve," she said. "Picture time."

She opened her door, and then everyone decided to follow. Probably better to stick together, than leave one alone.

They all hustled out and stood away from the truck as Mr. Belfield lifted the bear flop up with the shovel from the back of the truck. Crista snapped photos as Mr. Belfield laid the rank pattie on the hood of the truck. Then he spread it around a little. "Want to give him a full smell," he said. Everyone wrinkled their noses with disgust. Crista was interested. This was something she'd never seen before and never would have thought of.

Pictures taken, everyone rushed back into the truck and Mr. Belfield started it up.

"Do you think we'll find the sheriff soon?" Crista

asked. She checked her camera again and endured a barrage of questions from Lindy.

"We'll see," Mr. Belfield said above Lindy's chattering. "All we can do is see."

·17·

The Winding Road

The road wound around and up the mountain, getting steep in places. Mr. Belfield pointed out several more flops and got out and checked each one. Everyone gathered around, not comfortable being in the truck without Mr. Belfield there. He inspired confidence and didn't seem afraid in the least. He poked around in the flops with a stick and pronounced them both older than the one on the hood. As the smell sifted around in the air and wafted over their truck and the cab, Crista realized she hardly noticed it anymore. When she asked Mr. Belfield about this, he said, "Yeah, you soak in it, and after awhile you don't notice a thing."

They drove slowly, methodically through the woods, stopping frequently and listening. Strangely, none of the men from the circus or the police station came into sight. Soon they reached a dead birch lying across the road and Mr. Belfield stopped and got out again. He wasn't looking at the birch, though. He took the group over to a rotted log which was lying next to the birch.

Stooping down, he raked at the rot, and the bark and wood fiber fell off in chunks. "He's been here," Mr. Belfield said. "See the claw marks."

Indeed, claw marks raked all over the log and upon closer inspection, Crista realized it had been turned over. She took more pictures of the log and of the group gathered around. She was glad she had bought three more rolls of film the day before in anticipation of more photos, so she had plenty—over a hundred exposures.

The bear had stuck his paws into the loose wood, then dug at the log, breaking it open and revealing numerous bugs and worms on the inside.

"Bear like this one likes insects, larvae, grubs, all the kinds of things that grow on the underside of a log when it rots," Mr. Belfield said. "This is recent too." He laid his hand on it. "See," he said, "it's still wet. Not dried out from the sunlight. Plenty of that here. The bear's been here in the last twenty-four hours, I'd say."

Crista noticed Steve was writing everything down on his pad. She took more close-ups of the log. The air was warmer in the woods, now, and insects buzzed around like dive-bombers.

Mr. Belfield stood up again, pulled out his pistol, checked it, then shoved it back into its holster. "I know this guy is not an attack type of critter, but he's getting used to the outdoors. Probably likes it. He will not go gently into that good night, or their arms, I don't think."

"You mean, they'll really have to shoot him?" Jeff asked. He glanced at Crista and she returned his gaze uneasily.

"No. If they have the right equipment, they can get him without a shot fired," Mr. Belfield explained. "But these are country folk around here, not pros. And you did say there's people from the circus. Some of them, as you've said, aren't too happy about this bear being number one in the show."

"What can we do?" Crista asked for the hundredth time.

"Keep on going," Mr. Belfield said, leading them back to the truck. "And look for more signs. He's been here, walking around here a lot. So he knows the area now and feels comfortable with it. He's getting a taste for freedom, that's for sure. Instincts all flooding back into him. He could probably do right well out in the wilderness."

As Mr. Belfield spoke, Crista thought about his words. What if the bear was set free? Where would Cal Turner do such a thing? And would that be wise? For the first time, she made up her mind to talk to Mr. Turner about it—if all turned out well.

Once more everyone jumped into the truck and Mr. Belfield fired it up. As they came over a rise at the top of a little valley, he stopped one more time and took a long look out over the hood of the truck. There were puddles of water on the road and once more he stepped out to take in what was there. Everyone crowded around him as he stooped and showed them the bear claw etched into the mud on the edge of the water. "He drank some here," Mr. Belfield said. "At least this morning. See how the claw marks are a little dry. If it was older, there would be crack lines in them as the dirt pulls back with the sun on it. This one is real fresh."

Mr. Belfield stood and took the wind's direction one more time, then said, "Shhhhhh!"

Everyone stopped. For a moment, Crista thought he'd heard the bear. But then she noticed squirrels scurrying back and forth in the woods and birds singing for the first time. It was a happy, friendly noise in the woods.

"He's not here now, though," Mr. Belfield said.

"How do you know?" Steve asked. Crista could tell the reporter had gotten more nervous the closer they got to the top of the mountain. No one knew where all this was going and everyone felt more on edge. Mr. Belfield was a good guide, but he sure had a way of putting a heavy case of the heebie-jeebies into your gizzard!

"Listen!" Mr. Belfield whispered.

Everyone lapsed into silence and listened intently. It sounded like the regular old woods to Crista. She'd been out here a thousand times when it sounded like that. There were occasional crickets, some flies in the air, and birds tweeting here and there, fluttering through the trees, having little nip and tuck fights with one another.

"What?" Steve finally said, low and trembly.

"Don't you hear it?" Mr. Belfield asked. He smiled and waited. No one said anything. "The woods. You're in the middle of a joyful, unworried section of the woods. No one's fearful. No bad animals around. That's why it's noisy. Now you get that bear lumbering into the area, suddenly everything'll go real quiet. It's the hunter's nightmare—when he knows something's there, but he can't see it. He can feel it in his bones, but he can't see a thing. It's then that whatever it is jumps up and bites into his neck!"

Everyone stood still, shivered, and laughed nervously.

"Well, in a minute, back to the safety of the truck, girls and boys. We've got a ways to go yet. But first, the snare. Get those hot dogs, Crista!"

·18·
Sizzling Dogs!

Crista ran to the truck, wondering what Mr. Belfield was up to now. She grabbed the bag of hot dogs and hustled it over to the little group.

"Who's got a cigarette lighter?" Mr. Belfield said.

Everyone looked at everyone else. "We don't smoke cigarettes," Lindy declared. "They're skungy."

"Skungy?" Crista cried. "Skungy!"

"It's a cross between skunk cabbage and grunginess," Lindy said, folding her arms.

Steve said, "Sorry, I don't smoke either."

"What's the chief Boy Scout rule?" Mr. Belfield asked, reaching into his pocket and pulling out a little blue Bic lighter.

No one knew what the Boy Scout rule was.

"What am I dealing with here, city slickers?" Mr. Belfield said. "The main rule—the motto, I think they call it—is 'Be prepared.' Never go out into the woods without a fire source, ladies and gentlemen, or you're in big trouble. Now what's the second thing we need?"

Everyone looked again at everyone else. Crista had no idea what to think now, but she liked Mr. Belfield's style. He was a good teacher. The old man grinned through the gray hair of his goatee and shook his head with mock astonishment. "Remind me never to go alone in the woods with the likes of all of you," he said. "I'd be done for."

He drew a pocketknife out of his jacket pocket and opened it. It was a long-bladed knife with about ten parts, including a little fork and spoon. "A knife, ladies and gents. You never go into the woods without fire to keep warm and cook, and a knife to prepare the wood for the fire and do plenty of other things, including clean fish, skin rabbit, and trap squirrel. It's the most basic principle of survival and you kiddos wouldn't last a day out here if there wasn't civilization forty yards away to rescue you outta trouble. Now with this here knife, we are gonna make us a little bear bait."

Everyone watched as Mr. Belfield pulled down a branch from the oak tree closest to him and broke off several long slim shoots from the main branch. Handing them around, he said, "Strip 'em and get them cleaned off so we can poke the dogs through a few."

They all worked to get the sticks as clean and straight as possible. Crista grinned at Lindy who worked on hers as if it was the last branch on earth. The little girl was really excited, as much as Jeff and she were, and it made Crista feel happy that she was there. Somehow having Lindy along always made her feel a little motherly.

With five sticks all prepared, Mr. Belfield said, "All right, now we poke one dog on each and stick them in the ground over here in a little circle." He led them over to a patch of moss and kicked it with his feet. "Push them down in here," he said, "but first stick the hot dog on the end—horizontally not vertically." He demonstrated, sticking the hot dog through the middle instead of lengthwise. "We want to make it as easy on old Vic as possible."

He set the stick with the hot dog on the edge of the mossy area. He made it hang slightly over the road. Everyone followed suit. The five hot dogs sat in a row along the dirt edge. Finally Mr. Belfield held up the lighter and flicked it, turning back to the hot dogs. "We singe each one. That sends up the aroma right into the air. Bear can smell it a mile away if the wind's right, and it's right here—if he's up that way. We'll set up a couple of these little hot dog stands along the way and see if we can't drum us up a bear!"

Mr. Belfield singed the first hot dog, then he let Crista, Steve, Jeff, and finally Lindy try it. When Lindy was done, she announced, "I could eat one right now."

"Yes, I know," Mr. Belfield said. "But these are for the bear. There'll be other hot dogs for the likes of you." He gave her a friendly flick on the head and then led everyone back to the truck.

Crista said, "Let me get some pictures of the hot dogs now before we go. Don't anyone leave now!"

Mr. Belfield gave her a little hug around the shoulders. "Don't worry. We aren't going to leave you out here alone."

Crista took three snaps from different angles of the five hot dogs. Then she took one final shot of the group lolling on the back of the truck and gazing around at the woods. Lindy gave her a thumbs up as she took a final shot.

"All right, I'm done," Crista said, packing the camera away and ambling back over to the group. She didn't like the feeling of turning her back to the woods, as if the bear might roar out and breathe smoke and fire down her neck. But she tried to act brave and unconcerned.

They continued up the road, and every hundred yards they set up one or two more hot dogs. After getting a dozen out in four little "stands," as Mr. Belfield called them, he said that was enough. Then he pulled the truck onto a little rise and turned around. Driving back past the first stand, he stopped and gave a final lecture.

"Now if he comes this way, and I think there's a good chance he will, we've got to let him eat. Once he's gotten a taste of these," he looked at the bag, "these Oscar Meyer all beef wieners, he'll be sure to want more. Probably not getting real good eatin' out here, even if he does like it. So he'll sniff them on the wind. He should come right down this way. Hopefully he won't be traveling so fast that he won't stop for a bite. So we've got to get on the lookout. And that brings up the third item I brought along which you sometimes need in the woods—though not as much as the others. And that's a good pair of eyes."

He pulled out a small pair of binoculars and handed them around. When Crista took a turn, she turned around in the cab, looking out the back window. She wondered what Mr. Belfield was planning to do, but for now she felt safe in the cab of the truck.

It was then that Mr. Belfield flicked on one of the radios in the front of the truck under the dashboard. Crista knew it was not a CB, but she'd never seen one like it before. When it crackled on, Mr. Belfield said, "It's a police band radio. Picks up what the cops are talking about. We'll see what's going on from their point of view and see if we can get them a message on the CB. I can't talk on the police radio—that's illegal—but I can listen in. And maybe find out what's going on."

The voice of a dispatcher came on and an officer responded, saying he was pulling over someone in a blue Chevy for speeding. He gave the license plate number.

"Just police chatter," Mr. Belfield said. "The sheriff might have a radio along where they are now. A lot of cops now have them clipped on their shoulders so they can talk anytime, anywhere. They might be too far away to call home, but I don't think so. We may pick up something."

Mr. Belfield set the parking brake on the truck and turned off the engine. "Now we wait," he said. "Are you ready to take some more pictures, Crista?"

"Yes, sir," she replied.

"What are you going to do with them?"

Crista glanced at Steve a moment, then said, "If we get some of the bear, Steve is hoping to use them in the paper."

"Bucks County paper?" Mr. Belfield said.

"Right," Steve answered. "It's my first week as a reporter."

"Good for you. I read that paper every day," Mr. Belfield said. "I'll look for your byline."

"Thanks." Steve glanced back at Crista and she smiled, giving him a boost by raising her eyebrows and making a face. She could tell he was feeling a little bedraggled now with nothing big happening.

Jeff stepped out the side door with the binoculars and scanned the woods. Lindy stood next to him. Mr. Belfield fiddled with different bands on the police radio, trying to find something interesting. Crista and Steve talked more about what the article would say.

"The main thing is the bear," Steve said. "If we don't see him or anything, there's no story."

"We'll see him," Crista said. "I can feel it. My stomach is full of butterflies."

"Yeah, so is mine."

Suddenly Jeff stuck his head back in the truck. "We have visitors."

Mr. Belfield jumped out and looked upwind. Two young men were walking down the road with rifles over their shoulders. They were dressed in jeans and boots. Crista did not recognize them, but they were not police officers, that was for sure. They stepped out of the dark part of the woods, and sunlight caught them on the cheeks and forehead. They did not look friendly.

"Ho!" Mr. Belfield cried, waving to the two young men. They sped up the pace and soon stepped within talking distance of the truck.

·19·

The Larby Boys

Crista listened from the truck as Mr. Belfield and the two young men spoke. The boys were of medium height, slim, dark complected. She knew right away they had to be the Larby boys, although they did not introduce themselves as such. Jeff said to Crista and Lindy, "Let's find out what these guys are up to."

Crista opened the door and jumped down to join Jeff and Lindy. Steve sat up in the front seat, still writing down notes. Crista followed Jeff and Lindy was right behind them. The air around them was cool and she shivered a little. It was getting toward late in the afternoon now, and if something didn't happen soon, it would be dark.

"We saw the bear about an hour ago—at a distance," the older-looking of the two boys said. "He was traveling fast and we couldn't keep up."

"Someone got off shots earlier," Mr. Belfield said.

"Yeah, it was too far, though. Couldn't get him in my sights. Just shot wild." The older-looking fellow was doing all the talking. His cheeks were covered with a hairy down, not really a beard yet, and several pimples. He was dirty, too, and scowled and spit each time he said something.

142

"You shouldn't be shooting at that bear," Crista suddenly broke in. "He hasn't hurt anyone."

"That's not what we hear," the boy said. "Someone got chewed up real bad."

"It was a fake," Crista replied immediately. She turned to Jeff, "Tell them what we found." She wanted to see their response, what they would say when they learned their father was about to be exposed.

Jeff shifted on his feet, though, and only said, "We think someone caused the accident that turned over the bears' trailer."

"Oh, yeah, and what did you find?" The taller boy leaned a little closer. He was menacing and mean looking, and he obviously knew some of the details of what had happened. Crista realized it was bad strategy even to mention it.

Steve came up behind them and said, "We need to talk to the sheriff about it. Do you know where he is?"

"You can talk to us," the boy said. "We'll take it to him."

"No, we'll talk to the sheriff." Mr. Belfield's calm, commanding voice let the two boys know the matter was closed. "Where are you two headed?"

"Just down the road. Anyway, none of your business where we're headed." He gave Crista and Jeff an angry look, then checked his rifle and passed on. "That bear needs to be destroyed," he said. "It's vicious and shouldn't be in the circus in the first place."

"Is your name Larby?" Crista asked as they went by.

"What's it to you?"

"Just wanted to know." She stepped back a little as the young men passed her. The older one glared at her, then spit onto the ground.

"Don't you go shootin' at that bear," Mr. Belfield warned. "That's an almost tame bear, and he doesn't mean anyone any harm."

"We'll be the judge of that." The boy ran his hand over his greasy-looking hair and spit again. His brother, who had still not said a thing, spit too. They were obviously not planning to let this thing sit. "If that bear even looks at us wrong, we'll take him out. We're part of the circus, too, and we know how to deal with our own."

"I'm not so sure of that," Crista murmured under her breath, barely daring to look up into the older boy's squinty, surly eyes and face.

When they had passed on down the road, Mr. Belfield said, "They're going to be trouble."

"They can kill the bear!" Crista exclaimed. "Isn't there anything we can do?"

"Get to the sheriff," Mr. Belfield said. "He's probably coming this way, so I'll get on the CB and see if I can pick up someone with the crew."

Everyone walked back to the truck and got in. Anger sizzled on each face. Lindy looked like she wanted to bite off the Larby boys' noses. In the truck, Mr. Belfield picked up the microphone for the CB and began to radio. "C-Q. C-Q. This is Frank Belfield on the mountain looking for the circus bear. Anybody on this channel?"

Static erupted as he let the speaker button go and no one answered immediately. After several more tries, he switched channels. A man's voice came on. "This is the Headless Horseman, traveling up 590 in an eighteen wheeler. What's your handle?"

Mr. Belfield replied, "The White Hunter, Headless Horseman. You in a semi coming up 590? Did you pass a lot of cars with some police vehicles mixed in on the right?"

"Yessirree. Bunch of men standing around. Just passed it. About ten of them. What's going on, White Hunter?"

Mr. Belfield explained about the bear and the search. Then he said, "Headless Horseman, have you talked to anyone on another channel who might be in the search?"

"No one, White Hunter. Wish I could help. Sounds like you got a real problem. But I'll be out of your range in a couple minutes. Just passed the dam on the way to the main highway up to Hawley and Honesdale. Good luck!"

"Keep on truckin', Headless. Over and out." Mr. Belfield switched to another channel and tried the same kind of patter. No one responded. Lindy stood up in the cab and looked out the rear window through the binoculars.

Crista said, "If they're all coming in like it sounds, maybe we can drive out there and talk to the sheriff right now."

Mr. Belfield nodded and glanced at Steve, then the others. "Well, you want to leave and try to get to the sheriff on the other side of the mountain?"

"You could go down the trail, I bet," Jeff suddenly said. He looked at Crista. "By the Love Tree and all. It's wide enough, don't you think? And it intersects with this road down aways toward the Semms', right?"

Crista nodded. "It would be the fastest way."

"All right," Mr. Belfield said. "But..."

"Wait! Wait!" Lindy yelled. "I think I see something!"

Everyone turned around. Crista took the binoculars and peered through them up the trail past the sticks with the hot dogs. Bushes rustled a little, but she couldn't see what it was. It was getting toward evening and the sun was lower in the sky.

Mr. Belfield slowly opened his door and stepped out. "Everyone real quiet!" he whispered. "It might be a doe. Might be something else."

Everyone knew what "something else" meant!

Crista trained the binocs on the bushes, watching intently, her heart pounding. Jeff sat up next to her and she could tell he was as scared as she was. Mr. Belfield slunk down along the side of the truck, and Steve slowly opened his door.

Lindy asked, "Is it him? Is it the bear?"

Crista answered, "I still don't see him. But the leaves are rustling. It's got to be something. Here, take the binoculars." She handed them to Lindy. "I'm getting my camera out." Lindy took them from her hand, and Crista brought up the camera, adjusted it, and sighted through the viewfinder. Mr. Belfield crouched down at the back edge of the rear tire, watching.

Everyone seemed to stop breathing as the branches in a little thicket shook again. It was less than ten feet from the hot dogs, about fifty feet from the rear of the truck. Crista aimed the camera and watched, her heart almost exploding inside her.

"Come on, move out you little beary-poo!" she heard Jeff say.

Lindy touched Crista's leg and put her hand into a pocket. "I'm really scared now," she said.

Crista was surprised.

Then they all saw it. A huge brown paw, grizzled, flashed in the air and mashed down the branches of the thicket. It moved slowly, lumbering, sniffing every step. He had his nose high in the air, craning his neck, swiveling around and peering this way and that. Surely he saw the truck.

A second later, it stood in the road. The bear was huge, the same one that had been in the Semms' front yard. It turned and, with two tiny brown eyes, seemed to be looking in their direction. It sniffed the air and turned around. It had to see the truck, Crista thought. Or smell them all, flop or no flop.

She snapped her first picture.

The bear stepped into a spot where the sunlight shone through. Its grizzled fur looked almost silver in the stark sunlight. A long red tongue shot out and the bear stepped slowly toward the hot dogs, sniffing and watching the truck.

Mr. Belfield crept back inside the truck and said to Steve, "Get in, we have to be ready to go if he charges."

"He won't," Lindy whispered.

Crista took several more shots.

Mr. Belfield said low, "We're downwind from him now, so he hasn't gotten a real good whiff of us. But he'll get it soon. That's when we find out how tame he really is."

"But can't he smell us on the hot dogs and stuff?" Jeff asked. He was hunched down, watching the bear through the binoculars now. Lindy had squeezed between Crista and Jeff so that she pressed against both of them as they eyed the bear through the camera and binoculars.

Mr. Belfield answered, "He's used to humans enough that he's obviously not afraid of them at a distance. Let's just watch."

The bear swatted the hot dogs to the ground, then took one into his mouth. Crista watched with fascination as he wisely pulled it off the stick.

"He's eating it just like we would," Lindy said. "Maybe he's really a man in a bear suit."

"Don't think so," Crista said. She snapped pictures, but the view was not very good through the rear window. Looking up at the roof a moment, she said to Mr. Belfield, "Could you open the sunroof so I can get better pictures?"

"Sure," Mr. Belfield replied. He pressed a button and the roof slid noisily backward. Instantly, the bear turned toward the truck and Crista could see the hair on its back ripple slightly, as if he felt afraid.

After a second looking around, though, he continued scarfing up the hot dogs. Crista popped through the roof and snapped several more pictures of the bear as he finished his appetizer and then turned, smelled the air one more time, and shambled toward the truck.

"He's coming this way!" Lindy said breathlessly.

"Be quiet," Crista hissed as she bent down through the sunroof. "We don't want to scare him away."

Mr. Belfield released the parking brake and then took the truck out of gear. With the hill in front of them, they could roll a ways before he needed to start it.

The bear stopped and pawed in front of him, but he was obviously hungry and not that concerned that humans were less than a hundred feet away. He shuffled down to the second stand of hot dogs and consumed them happily, slurping them up without even knocking the sticks down. He simply pulled each one off the stick and sucked it down in one chomp.

"He's real hungry," Mr. Belfield remarked. "Hunting isn't as good as we thought it was."

The bear drew closer and Mr. Belfield let the truck roll downhill. He didn't roll fast, though. He let the bear get less than forty feet away. The bear was chomping down the hot dogs with nerve now, as if no one else was present. Crista focused and shot, focused and shot.

"What do we do when he runs out of hot dogs?" Steve asked, as he drew a picture of the bear eating them.

Crista ducked down inside. "I can throw more out as we roll down the hill. Maybe we can lead the bear right to the sheriff."

"That's exactly what I was thinking," Mr. Belfield said. The bear ambled along, sniffing and drawing nearer to the truck. Jeff poked his head through the opening now, and soon Lindy squished between him and Crista.

Setting the bag of hot dogs on the roof, Crista said, "As soon as he finishes the last stand of hot dogs, what should I do, Mr. Belfield?"

"I'll roll a ways, then throw one out when the bear's lookin' at you. Make sure he sees it and he's got that nose in the air. He'll probably run down and grab it up and keep on coming. He's a lot hungrier than I thought. Probably hasn't had a square meal since he got away."

·20·

Hot Dogs
on the Road

When the bear had finished the last group of hot dogs, Crista threw the first wienie over the rear end of the truck. It tumbled then rolled and stopped. The bear stood on his rear legs and shadowboxed the air a moment, then sniffed. He seemed to have the scent because he plunked down on all fours and hiked up the road toward the hot dog, his whole body rippling and rolling with the muscles under the thick coat. He looked beautiful in the light, handsome and powerful.

A second later, the bear lapped up the lone hot dog with his tongue. Mr. Belfield stopped the truck and waited. They all sat about fifty feet down from the bear.

"Let him come toward you as I roll," Mr. Belfield said. "We won't have enough hot dogs otherwise. Keep him coming till he loses interest, then throw him one."

The truck rolled forward. The bear stood again, churned the air with his front legs, and looked around. After sniffing the air, he sank down again, loping along like a horse this time.

"He's coming fast," Jeff yelled. "Throw him one."

"Not yet," Crista said. "Let's let him get close so I can get a picture. You throw the hot dogs, Lindy. I'll take the shots."

The bear hurried forward, and Mr. Belfield kept the truck out ahead of him by about thirty feet. He let the grizzly get as close as twenty feet, then slowly edged forward and increased the gap. Crista snapped pictures furiously, getting every expression and look of the bear's face. "He's really cute," she said as Lindy threw out a hot dog and the bear quickly found it.

This time, though, the bear picked up the hot dog in a paw, knocked it into the air, and caught it in his teeth.

"Oh, look, he's playing," Lindy cried. Crista got two more snaps, one just as the bear threw the wienie into the air, and a second with his head back just before he caught it on the downstroke.

"This is great. Maybe he'll catch one if we throw it right to him," Crista said. "Can we try that, Mr. Belfield?" She ducked into the truck and spoke directly to the old man.

"He'll have to get pretty close," he replied. "But I can watch him. I'm not letting him crawl aboard, though."

"Jeff, you better throw this one!" Crista said as she squeezed back up through the roof.

"I can do it," Lindy protested. "I play T-ball, you know."

Jeff grinned. "Who am I to argue? Go ahead, Lindy. Hit him with your best shot!"

Mr. Belfield slowed down, just inching forward as the bear hustled up closer to the truck, sniffing and pawing the air, but acting for all the world like this was his usual way of being fed.

"Get ready!" Crista yelled, holding the camera in position. Lindy drew her arm back as if to throw a spiral football. A moment later, she threw. Up, up! It was right on course. But too far to the left. The bear leaped, tried to catch it, but missed. Immediately, as it rolled past him, he whipped around, scarfed it up, then turned, stood on his hind legs, and bellowed.

"Rrrrrrrrrrrrrr!"

"He wants me to do it again," Lindy cried.

"Do it!" Jeff said. Crista took two more pictures. Lindy pulled her arm back and got ready. The bear bounded forward on his hind legs, growling and snorting approval.

"He really digs this," Crista said, using a term she had often heard her mother use years ago when she meant someone enjoyed an activity. "Now this time hit him right!"

Lindy practiced hurling the hot dog forward with several pretend throws, then she threw it high and long.

The bear danced up on his hind legs, moving backward slightly. The hot dog was on target.

"Yo! Right in his teeth!" Jeff yelled. "Perfect!"

"He is one smart bear!" Crista said, as she took the photo the moment the bear chomped into the thrown wiener.

Mr. Belfield had his window down now and was on the CB. "Ten-four, ten-four. Anybody on the horn? This is White Hunter."

Crista heard the CB crackle. Then someone came on. "Ten-four, good buddy. Who are you?"

"We're up on the mountain with a bear. You with the search team?"

"Yessirree! We're all gathered down at the road. Where are you?"

"Coming down to the dump road. We've got the bear right behind us. We're feeding him hot dogs, and he's taking the bait. Look, there's a cabin and clearing out here. The Semms live there. We're going to lead the bear into the clearing. Can you get the bear trainer over there in fifteen minutes? We're leading the bear down. He seems happy to be catching hot dogs here. But we don't know how long he'll stick with us, and we don't have any equipment to restrain him."

"I'll see what I can do."

The truck moved forward again, and one more time the bear loped after them, very hungry indeed.

A second later, another voice came on the radio. "Say there, White Hunter. You're not gonna shoot my little ol' dancin' bear, are ya?"

"Who's this?" Mr. Belfield said.

"This is Cal Turner. I'm Vic's trainer. He won't hurt anybody."

"We know, Cal," Mr. Belfield said. "In fact, we may have some evidence for you to prove who's trying to do this bear in."

"Who's that?"

"Jon Larby."

Turner laughed. "Yeah, he's been trying to do me and my bears in for years now."

"His two sons are up here, though. You know that, right?"

Turner's voice took on a somber tone. "Don't let them near the bear. They'll do anything to get a shot at him."

"What about Jon Larby?"

"He's up here somewhere with his gun, too. We got to keep our eyes open. Say, you don't have a megaphone or anything on this radio of yours?"

"Sure do. On the side of the truck."

As Crista listened, she suddenly understood what Mr. Turner wanted to do. He was going to talk to the bear through the CB. There was a little speaker in the cab with a wire connection. Mr. Belfield passed it up to Jeff and said, "Point it at Vic and let's keep going. Let Mr. Turner talk to him."

"You ready there, Mr. Turner?"

"Anytime."

"Go ahead. You're on the bear!"

The grizzly lapped up one more hot dog, and this time he performed a little somersault afterwards.

"He's getting happy," Crista said. "Let's keep going."

Mr. Turner's voice came on the megaphone CB attachment. "Vic! Hey, Vic, you hear me there?"

The bear immediately perked up and acted as if he understood the voice. Mr. Belfield said into the microphone, "He's got your number, Cal!"

Crista took more pictures as the bear continued to listen and cock his head as if unsure of where the voice could be coming from. The truck kept on rolling down the road, picking up speed, and the bear lumbered on behind them.

"This is your buddy, Daring Dan, Vic. Hear me?"

The bear cocked his head and stopped.

"Everything's all right, Vic. Just follow this truck and get as many of those dogs as you want. But we'll be comin' for you. Hear that?"

Vic listened to the voice. "Vic, show them you know what's going on. Turn around and dance. Dance, boy!"

Immediately, Vic rose on his hind legs and pirouetted—a bit clumsily, but he was definitely dancing. Everyone cheered. Cal kept talking to the bear and had him do two more tricks.

As they started down the road again, Lindy threw more hot dogs over and the grizzly snapped them up like pills. They reached the curve that led down to the

Semms' yard, and Crista watched as the first of the sheriff's cars pulled into the lot. Others were on the road.

Making the turn toward the Semms' house, the bear followed along as if a force impelled him. Mr. Turner kept purring into the CB about how good Vic was acting and that he'd be home soon and that all was well. Lindy had less than one pack of hot dogs left now, and Crista worried that they'd run out before the sheriff and circus people had time to get up whatever equipment they needed to guide the bear into a cage.

In another minute, Crista spotted the roof of the Semms' house. In another ten seconds, she saw that Johnny and Nadine had come out and stood in the yard. Johnny held his gun, but it wasn't up. Crista knew he was not about to fire now, not when a whole line of cars and trucks were coming in behind the bear. She saw the sheriff's car already parked in the yard.

Vic kept following, keeping his nose to the ground now and looking a little nervous. Whatever car Cal Turner was in must have been getting closer, because Crista noticed the signal was stronger.

"Throw the whole pack," Mr. Belfield said to the three kids. "We want him to stop. But keep a couple just in case." The truck clanked to a halt on the dusty curve.

Men with a net and long sticks stood at one end. They were all circus people. The sheriff and his men had drawn their guns and stood at the other, down from Vic and Mr. Belfield's truck. Vic tore into the little pile of hot dogs that Jeff had thrown out together.

Seconds later, there was a shout down the road and the repaired bear trailer with the two other bears in it rattled down toward them. When it stopped, Cal

Turner jumped out and walked toward Vic, now sitting in the road licking his paws.

As Cal walked forward, Crista snapped more pictures from the truck. "Vic, Vic, it's me! Your best friend!" Mr. Turner called. He was wearing an Australian bush hat this time, folded up and buttoned on one side. The bear looked around and roared a moment, as if in greeting.

"Wow, we've really got him!" Crista said. "And he's all right."

Lindy jumped up and down in the cab, her head poking through the roof. "I want to pet him! Can I pet him?"

Mr. Belfield jumped out and said to Steve, "Let's get this evidence to the sheriff right away." They circled around and began to confer with the sheriff, showing him the evidence they had.

Meanwhile, Cal Turner advanced. Vic continued licking his paws and acting as if nothing had happened. Crista took in everything as Mr. Belfield and Steve talked to the sheriff. They gestured up the road. A moment later, the sheriff took the bag of evidence and put it in his car, then started down the road.

Crista sighed a sigh of relief. It looked like the whole caper was over. Cal Turner was stepping to within ten feet of his dancing grizzly. He kept talking and reaching out to the bear in a friendly way. He held a muzzle in his left hand.

He had gotten close enough to throw the muzzle over Vic's head, when a shot suddenly rang out and a severed tree limb fell down. The bullet tore into the trees behind the bear on the other side of the road. It had obviously been aimed at Vic!

"Down!" the sheriff and several other men yelled.

Crista slumped back into the truck with Lindy and Jeff. "Someone's shooting at Vic!"

As the men moved in the direction of the woods, Vic jumped up and tore off at a gallop toward the trees behind the Semms' cabin. Cal Turner shouted something, and a second later, another shot ripped through the trees.

"What's going on?" Jeff yelled.

"I bet it's the Larby boys!" Crista cried. Jeff and Crista peeked up above the edge of the window of the truck to the outside. The police hadn't taken anyone, though, and as Crista turned, she saw the bear disappear into the trees.

"Come on, Cal," Mr. Belfield shouted, as he ran back toward the truck. "Into the truck!"

Mr. Turner ran up to the six-wheeler and climbed inside. Steve squeezed in with him. Mr. Belfield took off toward the place where Vic had gone into the trees. Meanwhile, the sheriff and several men ran off into the woods where the shots had come from.

"They're trying to get Vic so scared he does something bad and then they'll have to shoot him," Lindy yelled above the commotion.

"That's what I think," Mr. Belfield responded, as the truck crunched to a stop by the trees.

Cal Turner said, "The sheriff will get those two boys. They can't be far. Stupid! I can't believe they'd be this stupid."

"Well, it looks like they've got Larby," Mr. Belfield said, motioning to the group of men still on the road. Crista looked back and saw a police officer take Larby by the arm and shove him into one of the patrol cars.

"No one out of the truck now!" Mr. Belfield commanded as he wheeled around the yard. "Cal, this is your show."

"Bring up the other two bears," Cal Turner yelled as he jumped out of the truck. "And somebody get those boys and don't let them shoot those rifles again!"

Cal and Mr. Belfield stood outside the truck by the edge of the woods where Vic had plunged back in. Mr. Turner yelled Vic's name several times, and then shook his head. "I can't believe we let him get away!"

"Maybe we didn't," Mr. Belfield replied. "Crista, give me those last few hot dogs. And get your camera ready."

The three kids watched through the sunroof. Steve sat up in the front seat still taking notes. Mr. Turner and Mr. Belfield stepped into the woods after singeing the hot dogs and laying them on the ground about thirty feet from the truck. Crista got ready to take pictures. The man driving the big cage trailer drove right into the middle of the yard. Everyone else spread out and stayed on the cabin side of the field. No one wanted to go near that bear!

"Do you think they'll keep shooting at Vic?" Crista asked. She, Lindy, Jeff, and Steve sat in the truck, unwilling to move. The windows were down. It was close to dusk. The sun beamed its rays wide across the yard, throwing dark shadows everywhere.

Jeff said, "No, they'll get them. They have to get them. Shooting like that in broad daylight is about as stupid as you can get. They must have the brains of Vic himself."

"Vic has a smarter brain," Lindy said angrily.

Everyone turned toward the woods. The policemen and other circus people stood back in a large semicircle, their guns at the ready.

A moment later, Crista heard loud barking.

"Dump dogs!" Lindy suddenly cried. Ten mongrels romped out of the woods, running hungrily toward the hot dogs.

"Oh, no, we can't let them get the food!" Crista cried.

"But what are we gonna do?" Jeff asked.

"Stop them!"

Crista crunched down into the cab and opened the door. She knew it was dangerous, but there was little hope of flushing Vic out of the woods with real dump dogs there and the hot dogs gone. Furthermore, the dump dogs might scare the bear away for good!

"But the bear's out there!" Jeff yelled.

"And the Larby boys, too," Steve added.

"So what!" Lindy yelled as she followed Crista out the door.

Crista ran toward the dump dogs. The camera banged back and forth on her chest. She stooped to pick up a stick and wave it at them. Lindy, Jeff, and Steve were right behind her.

"Get out of here!"

"Go!"

"Scram!"

"Run!"

The dogs stopped twenty feet from the hot dogs, panting and peering at them with hot, yellow eyes. Every one of them looked like some canine thug. Most had deep scars and ugly marks. Crista had rescued Rontu and Tigger from this very crew—but Crista's dogs weren't here now and could do nothing to help.

Crista waved at them again, yelling. Together with Steve, Lindy, and Jeff they heaved their sticks at the dogs, dispersing them. Moments later, the dogs lurched back into the woods, a mass of barking and tails between legs.

"Well, that does that!" Jeff said, grinning at Crista.

Crista said, "Good!" She turned around and stopped dead on the dirt. There, not twenty feet from her, stood Vic on all fours, his mouth open, tiny brown eyes staring.

"Oh, boy," Lindy whispered. "Now we're really in trouble!"

·21·

In Too Deep to Quit!

The bear rose up on his hind legs, threw his head back, and roared. Steve and Jeff slowly stepped back, then Jeff grabbed Crista by the collar and Steve pulled back Lindy.

"Just go real slow," Steve said.

Crista slowly lifted the camera. "It's okay, Vic," she said. "It's just me. We won't hurt you."

The bear sat back on his seat as if resting. His paws slowly descended to his sides, butterfly-like. He looked just like Winnie the Pooh about to steal honey from a honey jar. Crista lifted the camera to her eyes and looked through the viewfinder. Suddenly Vic stood up again, startled. He lifted his paws and rolled his head back. Then he roared. Crista almost fell back. Vic was even bigger than Val had been that day. And this time she wasn't on a horse.

Somehow she kept her nerve, though, and pressed the shutter button. Once. Wind. Twice. Wind again. Three times. "Just hold it there, Vic," she said as if she were photographing him in her living room.

She focused the camera one more time as she backed up. Vic shook his head, looked around, and roared again. Crista snapped a fourth time. It was perfect.

Vic's limbs splayed out. His mouth open, his head back in a roar. What a sight!

The bear looked both ways, first at the woods, then at the hot dogs. Finally, he came down on all fours and padded over to the little pile. In a matter of seconds it was gone!

Crista snapped pictures as fast as she could, checking to see how much of the roll she had left. But that one picture was the prime shot of all time, the one in a hundred that might make it into the papers! If only it turned out!

Out of the corner of her eye, she saw Nadine and Johnny hurrying across the field. Johnny had his rifle up.

Crista yelled, "No, don't shoot! We're all right."

The sheriff and the others began moving in. Cal Turner and Mr. Belfield emerged from the woods behind the bear.

"Easy now, Vic. Easy," Mr. Turner said. He had a whip in his hand this time and what appeared to be Vic's choke collar and a muzzle to put over his head and cover his nose and mouth. No one else drew closer than a hundred feet.

Nadine called to Crista, "Get a Pulitzer prize-winning shot, Crista!"

Crista grinned and kept shooting.

Cal Turner, backed up by Mr. Belfield with his gun out, moved in on the bear. Vic just whimpered, licked his chops and his paws, and waited. He was the most docile-looking creature in the whole gathering.

As Mr. Turner moved in and Mr. Belfield backed him up, there was a sudden rustling of the bushes behind the bear. The two Larby boys stepped out, their rifles at their shoulders just a few feet away from Crista and the others.

"Put your guns down!" ordered the sheriff. "Now!"

"That bear's a menace," one of them yelled. They both kept their guns aimed at the bear.

With a whoop, Jeff ran toward them, then Steve and Lindy quickly followed. They hit the two boys high and low, knocking them down. Crista turned and got the whole thing on camera. Mr. Turner slipped the muzzle over Vic's head and brought him completely under control. The sheriff and his men moved in, and in less than ten seconds they pinned the Larby boys to the ground.

It was over in less than a minute. The sheriff led the two boys off in handcuffs as Mr. Turner led Vic into the middle of the yard toward the trailer with the other two bears.

A shout went up from everyone gathered as the grizzly stepped into the middle of the yard, subdued. But as the cheer went up, the bear suddenly stopped. As if on cue, he turned, looked at the crowd, then threw his paws up, joined them together over his head, and did a ballet pirouette.

Everyone shouted again and Vic performed a somersault, then stood and ran in place for a moment. Putting paws and hands together, Cal Turner began waltzing with Vic along through the crowd toward the trailer.

"He's a good old boy!" Mr. Turner shouted as he led Vic right up into the cage with the other two bears. "And you're all getting the reward!" he shouted to Mr. Belfield, Crista, and the others.

A tear dripped off Crista's chin as she took one last photo. "He should be free," she said. "Even if he is a great dancer!"

·22·

Cal Turner's Letter

Everyone started to climb into Mr. Belfield's truck, congratulating each other about the Larby boys, Vic, and everything else. But suddenly, Crista grabbed Lindy's hand and said, "Come on. We have one last thing to do."

"What?" Lindy cried just before being pulled off her feet. She tripped, but Crista had her hand and held her up.

"A little plea—for the bears!" Crista replied.

When they reached the bear trailer, all three bears sat inside looking bored and useless, certainly not very happy. Mr. Turner was just putting the lock in place and beginning to check the tires when Crista and Lindy walked up to him.

He turned and, upon seeing them, grinned. "You all did a great job out there," he said. "If there's anything I can do to repay you other than the reward..."

"There is," Crista said, looking at Lindy.

"All right, what?"

"Let the bears go!"

"Let them go?" Mr. Turner looked from Crista to Lindy with astonished surprise. "But this is my life."

"What about their lives?" Crista asked, motioning to the three bears. "I know they're your friends and

165

everything, Mr. Turner, and that you really love them, like your own kids. But if you let them go in Yellowstone or Glacier or one of the state parks, they'd be okay. Vic already proved that. And maybe they'd still dance for people, too. But they'd be free. You could visit them anytime, too."

Mr. Turner shook his head. "You mean like *Born Free* or something? You ask a hard thing. I'll think about it. I *am* getting too old for this game. But I can't guarantee anything." He looked at the bears affectionately. "They've been good friends." He turned back to the two girls. "Tell you what. I'll think about it and if we get out that way and I'm as tired as I am now, maybe it'll happen."

Crista shook his hand and Lindy offered hers. Then they ran back to where Mr. Belfield stood next to his truck. When Lindy and Crista climbed aboard, everyone wanted to know what was up. Crista just said, "We made a little suggestion to Mr. Turner. My and Lindy's secret."

No one talked that much, but Steve said, "Crista, we have to develop those pictures and see what they look like. This is a major story for our paper."

Crista fumbled inside her camera case and took out the two finished rolls and then rewound the roll inside the camera—she'd used up all thirty-six prints—and handed it to Steve. "You get them developed. I'm going home to sleep!"

* * *

Two stories by Steve Leonard appeared in the paper the next day, with a six-photo spread. The major one replayed the whole tale of Vic's escape and recapture and Crista's involvement with all her friends, including Mr. Belfield. There were captions on each picture. Crista's photo of Vic in the field, roaring and then dancing, made the front page. Inside were other pictures of the circus, Mr. Belfield, and the capture.

The second story headlined Johnny Junior's predicament and included another of Crista's pictures of Johnny, Nadine, and the twins. Steve jazzed it up with a recap of the story about the twins' birth at Christmastime and more about how Vic had hidden in the woods near their cabin. Everyone said Crista ought to be a journalist photographer and that Steve was headed for the big time. That Monday, Steve came by with a check for $400.

As Dr. Mayfield seated Steve in their living room, the reporter presented the check to Crista. "You earned it," he said.

"I know where this is going," Crista immediately answered.

"The bank?" her father wanted to know.

"No, for Johnny Junior's operation. And a new stove for the cabin. Everyone wants to give Nadine and Johnny the reward money, too. So this'll really help."

Steve added, "Oh, yeah! We've been getting a lot of calls about Nadine and Johnny Junior from people who want to help out. It looks like Johnny Junior's going to be all right."

* * *

Nadine wouldn't accept the money at first, but when Crista told her she'd taught her everything she knew about photography and, therefore, had really earned it, she accepted. She and Johnny went out and bought a new stove that week, and of course the rest went into savings in preparation for the operation. More money came in from interested folks around the lake area. In a matter of a week or so, Nadine and Johnny had more than enough money for everything. They scheduled the operation for the following week.

On Friday, the manager at the newspaper called and asked if Crista would like some more work as a photographer. When he found out she was only twelve, he said he was sorry to trouble her, but Crista suggested Nadine. Less than a week later Nadine had a part-time job as a stringer, allowing her to make the money needed for fixing up the cabin. And she would only have to work a minimal number of hours because she would be paid by the photo, not the hour. The newspaper would also provide transportation and babysitting when necessary, though Crista and Jeff said they could handle the babysitting.

* * *

Not too much later, Crista received a strange-looking letter in the mail. It was from Cal Turner. Excitedly, she ripped it open and read:

Dear Crista and Lindy,

I haven't been able to stop thinking about what you said to me. So I did it. We were in Ohio and there's a huge reserve there—an "in the wild" zoo where you drive around in cars and see the animals in their own habitats. I didn't have the courage to take Vic, Val, and Vinnie to Yellowstone, even though I'm sure they'd be able to make it there. But this is better. They're taken care of and, basically, they're free.

Thanks for making the suggestion. It was just what I needed to help me retire to my relatives' farm in Ohio—not far from my bears—and take it easy for the first time in fifty years. Val, Vinnie, and Vic are the big attraction now, I hear. They dance and dance. Must be in their blood.

Well, again, thanks. You've done everyone a service.

Sincerely,

Cal Turner,
Val, Vinnie, and Vic

There were three more pages, each with a bear print, and six pictures, one of each of the bears standing up pirouetting, and then three of Cal and the bears in their circus act.

Crista's eyes filled with tears later as she showed the letter to Jeff, Lindy, Steve, and finally Mr. Belfield. In the end, she made a collage of the bear pictures with the letter and bear prints as the centerpiece. She hung it up in the cabin over the main front window.

About the Author

Mark Littleton is the author of over 24 books, including the recent *Fillin' Up* in the Up Series of teen devotionals. He lives with his two children, Nicole and Alisha, in Columbia, Maryland.

The Action Never Stops in
The Crista Chronicles
by Mark Littleton

———

Secrets of Moonlight Mountain

When an unexpected blizzard traps Crista on Moonlight Mountain with a young couple in need of a doctor, Crista must brave the storm and the dark to get her physician father. Will she make it in time?

Winter Thunder

A sudden change in Crista's new friend, Jeff, and the odd circumstances surrounding Mrs. Oldham's broken windows all point to Jeff as the culprit in the recent cabin break-ins. What is Jeff trying to hide? Will Crista be able to prove his innocence?

Robbers on Rock Road

When the clues fall into place regarding the true identity of the cabin-wreckers, Crista and her friends find themselves facing terrible danger! Can they stop the robbers on Rock Road before someone gets hurt?

Escape of the Grizzly

A grizzly is on the loose on Moonlight Mountain! Who will find the bear first—the sheriff's posse or the circus workers? Crista knows there isn't much time...the bear has to be found quickly. But where, and how? Doing some fast thinking, Crista comes up with a plan...

Don't Miss Any of the
Addie McCormick Adventures!
by Leanne Lucas

The Stranger in the Attic

A vanishing visitor and secrets from the past... Can Addie and Nick put the puzzle together before something terrible happens to their friend Miss T.?

The Mystery of the Missing Scrapbook

A missing scrapbook, mysterious paintings, and an old letter lead Nick, Addie, and Brian on a heartstopping chase. Are they in over their heads this time?

The Stolen Statue

A movie star has been kidnapped and Miss T.'s statue has disappeared! Addie has all the clues... but can she put them together before it's too late?

The Chicago Surprise

When Addie and Nick catch a thief, what they discover about the culprit is much more than they bargained for!

The Mystery of the Skeleton Key

In Addie's family history, there's a "treasure" that no one can find! Will Addie be able to solve a mystery that's more than 100 years old?

The Computer Pirate

Someone is stealing information from the school's computer system! Addie's friend is the #1 suspect. Can she prove his innocence?

Find Adventure and Excitement in
The Maggie Series
by Eric Wiggin

Maggie: Life at The Elms

Maggie's father died at the Battle of Gettysburg, and
the man her mother is going to marry has a son who
Maggie just can't stand! She asks for permission to
live with her Grandpa in the deep woods of northern
Maine—at his special home, The Elms.

Little does Maggie know how much her life is about
to change—all because of an overfriendly hound dog,
a rude, sharp-tongued girl at a logging camp, clever
kitchen thieves in the night, and surprising lessons
about friendship and forgiveness.

Maggie's Homecoming

After two years in the deep woods with Grandpa,
Maggie is eager to return home. She and her step-
brother, Jack, must learn to get along—and to everyone's amazement, they do!

Before she has a chance to settle in to her new home,
Maggie is caught in another adventure. One Saturday
she and Jack decide to explore a long-abandoned farm-
house around the mountainside—only to find out the
place isn't abandoned after all...